SOCIO-ECONOMIC TRANSFORMATION OF INDIAN MUSLIMS

With Special Reference to Andaman Islands

SOCIO-ECONOMIC TRANSFORMATION OF INDIAN MUSLIMS

With Special Reference to Andaman Islands

Edited by
Swapan K. Biswas
Hema Bannerjee
Palash C. Coomar

KALPAZ

Published by

Kalpaz Publications
C-30, Satyawati Nagar,
Delhi – 110052
Ph.: 011-47034999, 9811692060
www.kalpazpublications.com
E-mail: kalpaz@hotmail.com

Distribution Network
gyanbooks.com
India, USA, Canada, UK, Australia, France

ISBN: 978-93-5722-276-1 (HB)

First Published, 2023

Printed at: Gyan Press, Delhi.

SOCIO-ECONOMIC TRANSFORMATION OF INDIAN MUSLIMS
Editors: SWAPAN K. BISWAS, HEMA BANNERJEE AND PALASH C. COOMAR

Contents

Part-Three
Socio-Cultural Diversity and Islands Muslims

Part-Four
Economy and Educational Perception in Islands Muslims

List of Contributors

1. Dr. Swapan K Biswas, Associate Professor & Head, Dept. of Political Science, MGG College , Mayabunder.
2. Prof. Muzaffar Assadi, Professor and Head, Department of Politics, Mysore University.
3. Prof. K.M. Sajad Ibrahim, Professor, Department of Politics, Kerala University, Kerala.
4. Dr. S.S. Sreekumar (Retd.), Associate Professor and Head, P G Department of Political Science, Jawaharlal Nehru PG Govt. College, Port Blair, Andaman.
5. Dr. Palash C. Coomar, Former Joint Director of Census Operations, Ministry of Home Affairs, Govt. of India.
6. Ms. Ricklina Roychowdhury, Junior Research Fellow, Anthropological Survey of India, Western Regional Centre, Udaipur, Rajasthan, India.
7. Dr. Hema Bannerjee, Associate Professor and Head, Department of Economics, Jawaharlal Nehru P.G. Govt. College, Port Blair, Andaman.
8. Dr. Swati Chakraborty, Research Consultant and Assistant Professor, Gurukul School, University of Delhi, Delhi.
9. Dr. Ajitha Narendran, Assistant Professor (S.G.), P.G. Department of Commerce, Jawaharlal Nehru. P.G. Govt. College, Port Blair, Andaman.
10. Dr. K. Rajmohan, Associate Professor and Head, Department of Commerce, Mahatma Gandhi Govt. College, Mayabunder, Andaman.

11. Dr. T. Prasad Rao, (Former) Assistant Professor (S.G.), Department of Historical Studies, Jawaharlal Nehru P.G. Govt. College, Port Blair, Andaman.
12. Dr. Kanwar Chanderdeep Singh, (Former) Assistant Professor (S.G.), Department of Historical Studies, Jawaharlal Nehru P.G. Govt. College, Port Blair, Andaman.
13. Smt. Anita Banerjee, (Former) Assistant Professor of Economics, Andaman Law College, Port Blair.
14. Dr. Sushim Kumar Biswas, Senior Teacher (Economics), Directorate of Education, A and N Administration.

1

Introduction

Swapan K Biswas

Islands society is the admixture of all religions /linguistic groups, who live peacefully with national integrity. Andaman society developed with the origin of Penal Settlement of British-India to settle convicted prisoners in 1858.This society has become a symbol of progress with social harmony and dignity for all minorities including six indigenous tribals. Muslims constitute 9 percent of the islands population, contributing in business and other social sectors along with other communities. In this vibrant society, the Muslims are cordial, liberal and progressive. The females are highly respected. To build a new society in the pre-independent India, Britishers needed equal ratio of both sexes in the newly built Penal Colony in Andaman. However, they faced the paucity of female members in Penal society.

The community-wise population movements in A and N Islands from 1858 to 1947 reflected that the convicted prisoners, who had been transported by the British, the Hindu and the Muslim were two major religious groups. The Penal Settlement of the British was started with 200 (who were freedom fighters of first war of Independence i.e. Sepoy Mutiny in 1857) prisoners in March 1858. In 1901, the population was recorded 24649, of which, the Muslim constituted 17.1 percent and Hindus 37.5 percent. The number of population of Muslim was remarkably increased from 17.1 percent in 1901 to 22.8 percent in 1931 and further increased its figure 23.7 percent in 1941. The transportation of Muslim in Andaman from mainland provinces was started with the Wahabbi movement launched as one of the earliest and most remarkable anti-British movements from Sylehat in Eastern part of Bengal to Peshawar in NWFP. Many Wahabis also joined the uprising against the British along with Sylehat and Western Provinces and also the places were Bhopal, Jaipur and Hissar. A number of trails were held and many of them were transported to the Andaman. (Ray and Chaudhury, 2002, pp. 16-17). However, the Hindu population in between two Census was not increased as it was in case of Muslim population. The causes behind the increased of Muslim population in Penal Settlement in between 1921–26 was, the number of the Moplah Muslim was that because of transported from Malabar region. Out of 1887 Moplahs, 714 were female. Later, their number was further increased due to hundred of family members of Moplah Muslims invited to join their husbands. "They were among the luckiest convicts. Each was encouraged to bring his family with him at Government expense and to move into the position of a self-supporters after only 3-4 months of imprisons terms. The Maplahs were allotted land close together, with schools for their children, usual assistance, as fishermen, petty traders or as cultivators with the right to occupancy under the newly amended Land Revenue Regulations" (Dhingra, 2005, p. 160). However, the Hindu-Muslim population ratio in 1941 was almost equal i.e. Muslims 8005 (23.71%) and Hindus 8427 (24.9%).

Apart from that a small number of Nicobaree tribals from Nicobar district converted from Christianity to Islam. In early twentieth century, the British allowed Yusuf Md. Jadwet, a Gujarati Muslim trader to start business in Car Nicobar. His company brought labourers and officials from Gujarat to run the establishment in Nicobar. As these staff stayed for a long time away from their homes, these young Muslim males started entering into marital relations with native girls. Most of these eligible bachelors or even married males who left their families in Gujarat started maintaining a family in Nicobar. (Biswas, 2015).

"Of late the number of Nicobari Muslims has increased in Car Nicobar and Nancowry islands with the advent of R Akoojee Jadwet during the British period.At that time some Nicobari certainly showed interest in embracing Islam partly because they were eager to adopt outside cultural traits including food habits and partly because they were spiritually enlightened and had access to certain privileges.Later, they also encouraged others to become Muslims."(Justine, 1990). There is a strong evidence that for a long time, the foreign nationals from Malaysia, Indonesia who arrived at these tiny isolated islands like Pilo-Milo, Kundul, Dering, Trinket in Nancowry group of islands were welcomed by local Nicobari families without the notice of local authority. Their frequent arrivals resulted in establishing intimate relations with local families as well as religious conversions. As Nicobaris were simple and liberal, they did not mind their daughters marrying non-Christians and converting to Islam.

The arrival of Muslims started in these islands during post-– independence to engage themselves in Government as well as private jobs. They were mostly from Kerala, Tamil Nadu, Uttar Pradesh, Gujarat, Bihar and West Bengal. After 90s a good number of Bengali Muslims have come as labourers, females as domestic help, petty businessmen (hawker, *Puchkawala*, Vegetable and fruits vender etc.), in city areas. Most of them were from 24 Parganas (South and North), Nadia, Midnapur, Malda and Murshidabad.

In Islam there are many sects are found around the Indian society. The majority are Sunni and Sia followers are small in number. In India around 3 percent are Sia. However, others are Wahabi group and Ahamadhi.

It has been observed from the Table1.1 that at the National Level, percentage of Muslim population to total population during 1991, 2001 and 2011 Censuses are 12.12 percent, 13.43 percent and 14.23 percent respectively.

In 1991 Census there were seven States/Union Territories where the percentage of Muslim population is higher than the National Average (12.12%). These States/Union Territories were

Table 1.1: India, States and Union Territories-wise Distribution of General and Muslim Population of Censuses – 1991, 2001 and 2011.

Country/States/Union Territories	Population			No. & Percentage of Muslim Population					
				1991		2001		2011	
	1991	2001	2011	No.	%	No.	%	No.	%
India	**846,421,039**	**1,028,737,436**	**1,210,854,977**	**101,596,057**	**12.12**	**138,188,240**	**13.43**	**172,245,158**	**14.23**
Jammu & Kashmir	NA	10,413,700	12,541,302	NA	---	6,793,240	65.23	8,567,485	68.31
Himachal Pradesh	5,170,877	6,077,900	6,864,602	89,137	1.70	119,512	1.97	149,881	2.18
Punjab	20,281,969	24,358,999	27,743,338	239,401	1.20	382,045	1.57	535,489	1.93
Chandigarh	642,015	900,635	1,055,450	17,477	2.70	35,548	3.95	51,447	4.87
Uttaranchal	7,050,634	8,489,349	10,086,292	NA	---	1,012,141	11.92	1,406,825	13.95
Haryana	16,463,648	21,144,564	25,351,462	763,775	4.60	1,222,916	5.78	1,781,342	7.03
Delhi	9,420,644	13,850,507	16,787,941	889,641	9.40	1,623,520	11.72	2,158,684	12.86
Rajasthan	44,005,990	56,507,188	68,548,437	3,525,339	8.00	4,788,227	8.47	6,215,377	9.07
Uttar Pradesh	132,061,753	166,197,921	199,812,341	24,109,684	17.30	30,740,158	18.50	38,483,967	19.26
Bihar	64,530,554	82,998,509	104,099,452	12,787,985	14.80	13,722,048	16.53	17,557,809	16.87
Sikkim	406,457	540,851	610,577	---	---	7,693	1.42	9,867	1.62
Arunachal Pradesh	864,558	1,097,968	1,383,727	---	---	20,675	1.88	27,045	1.95
Nagaland	1,209,545	1,990,036	1,978,502	20,642	1.70	35,005	1.76	48,963	2.47
Manipur	1,837,149	2,293,896	2,855,794	133,535	7.30	190,939	8.32	239,836	8.40
Mizoram	689,756	888,573	1,097,206	---	---	10,099	1.14	14,832	1.35
Tripura	2,757,205	3,199,203	3,673,917	196,495	7.10	254,422	7.95	316,042	8.60
Meghalaya	1,774,778	2,318,822	2,966,889	260,306	14.70	99,169	4.28	130,399	4.40
Assam	22,414,322	26,655,528	31,205,576	6,373,204	28.40	8,240,611	30.92	10,679,345	34.22
West Bengal	68,077,965	80,176,197	91,276,115	16,075,836	23.60	20,240,546	25.25	24,654,825	27.01

contd...

Jharkhand	21,843,911	26,945,829	32,988,134	NA	—	3,731,308	13.85	4,793,994	14.53
Odisha	31,659,736	36,804,660	41,974,218	577,775	1.80	761,985	2.07	911,670	2.17
Chhattisgarh	17,614,928	20,833,803	25,545,198	NA	—	409,615	1.97	514,998	2.02
Madhya Pradesh	48,566,242	60,348,023	72,626,809	3,282,800	5.00	3,841,449	6.37	4,774,695	6.57
Gujarat	41,309,582	50,671,017	60,439,692	3,606,920	8.70	4,592,854	9.06	5,846,761	9.67
Daman & Diu	101,586	158,204	243,247	9,048	8.90	12,281	7.76	19,277	7.92
Dadra & Nagar Haveli	138,477	220,490	343,709	3,341	2.40	6,524	2.96	12,922	3.76
Maharashtra	78,937,187	96,878,627	112,374,333	7,628,755	9.70	10,270,485	10.60	12,971,152	11.54
Andhra Pradesh	66,508,008	76,210,007	84,580,777	5,923,954	8.90	6,986,856	9.17	8,082,412	9.56
Karnataka	44,977,201	52,850,562	61,095,297	5,234,023	11.60	6,463,127	12.23	7,893,065	12.92
Goa	1,169,793	1,347,668	1,458,545	61,455	5.30	92,210	6.84	121,564	8.33
Lakshadweep	51,707	60,650	64,473	48,765	94.30	57,903	95.47	62,268	96.58
Kerala	29,098,518	31,841,374	33,406,061	6,788,364	23.30	7,863,842	24.70	8,873,472	26.56
Tamil Nadu	55,858,946	62,405,679	72,147,030	3,179,410	5.70	3,470,647	5.56	4,229,479	5.86
Pondicherry	807,785	974,345	1,247,953	52,867	6.50	59,358	6.09	75,556	6.05
Andaman & Nicobar Islands	280,661	356,152	380,581	21,354	7.60	29,265	8.22	32,413	8.52

Lakshadweep (94.30%), Assam (28.40%), West Bengal (23.60%), Kerala (23.30%), Uttar Pradesh (17.30%), Bihar (14.80%) and Meghalaya (14.70%). In Andaman and Nicobar Islands the proportion of Muslim population was 8.52 percent to the total population, which is lower than the National Average.

As per data collected during 2001 Census, there are eight States/Union Territories where the proportion of Muslim population is higher than the National Average. These States/Union Territories are Lakshadweep (95.47%), Jammu and Kashmir (65.23%), Assam (30.92%), West Bengal (25.25%), Kerala (24.70%), Uttar Pradesh (18.50%), Bihar (16.53%) and Jharkhand (13.85%). In the case of Andaman and Nicobar Islands, Muslim population covers 8.22 percent of the total population.

Census 2011 has recorded eight States/Union Territories where the percentage of Muslim population is higher than the National Average. These States/Union Territories are Lakshadweep (96.58%), Jammu and Kashmir (68.31%), Assam (34.22%), West Bengal (27.01%), Kerala (26.56%), Uttar Pradesh (19.26%), Bihar (16.87%) and Jharkhand (14.53%).

During 2011 Census Andaman and Nicobar Islands record 8.52 percent Muslim population of the total Island population. It is observed that proportion of Muslim population in the Bay Islands has increased steadily from Census 1991 to Census 2011from 7.60 percent to 8.52 percentat par trend of the National Level.

In all the three Censuses i.e. from Census 1991 to Census 2011, Uttar Pradesh scored top position in regard to the actual number of Muslim population in the country followed by West Bengal. Bihar ranks the third position, even after the bifurcation of Jharkhand State. Least number of Muslim populations is enumerated in Dadra and Nagar Haveli, Union Territory during 1991 and 2001 Census. But in 2011 Census, least number of Muslim populations is recorded in Sikkim.

According to British records and Census report prepared by them, revealed that Hindu, Muslims and Sikh were majority in number. The Muslims from almost all provinces, irrespective of

Table 1.2: Decadal Variation of Religion-wise Population in these Islands during1901-2011

Religion	1901	1931	1941	1951	1961	1971	1981	1991	2001	2011
Hindu (%)	9264 (37.5)	7618 (25.8)	8427 (24.9)	9294 (30.00)	32781 (51.58)	70143 (60.91)	121793 (64.52)	189521 (67.52)	264589 (69.23)	264313 (69.45)
Muslim (%)	4201 (17.1)	6719 (22.8)	8005 (23.71)	4783 (15.44)	7398 (11.64)	11655 (10.12)	16188 (8.57)	21354 (7.60)	29265 (8.22)	32425 (8.25)
Christian (%)	486 (1.97)	1461 (4.95)	2613 (7.73)	9494 (30.65)	17973 (28.28)	30342 (26.35)	48274 (25.57)	67211 (23.94)	77178 (21.66)	80581 (21.28)
Animist* (%)	8399 (34.07)	9955 (33.38)	11076 (32.80)	NA	NA	NA	NA	NA	NA	NA
Others	2299	3710	3647	7400	5396	3002	2486	2575	3100	2930
Total	**24649 (100.00)**	**29463 (100.00)**	**33768 (100.00)**	**30971 (100.00)**	**63548 (100.00)**	**115133 (100.00)**	**188741 (100.00)**	**280661 (100.00)**	**356152 (100.00)**	**380581 (100.00)**

*Animist are including Tribals of A and N Islands.

their language, culture developed a unique mixed local Hindustani Muslim culture and Urdu was the main language of communication of all communities. All official records in revenue, police departments were written in Urdu and English. Those males or females from other religion or faith who made union/marital relation with Muslim family had to follow Muslim faith and culture.

As per the Census 2011, it is found that Muslim constituted 8.25 percent of total population of these islands. However, many Social Science scholars observed that the Muslim population of these islands has been increased more than what census records stated. According to their opinion, a huge number of Muslims from Bengal, Bihar and Uttar Pradesh have immigrated as labourers and other activities in Port Blair and other islands. Even hundreds of Bangladeshi people also intruded illegally.

Place of Residence

Muslim among old settlers, the decedent of Ex-convicted are mostly residing in the heart of the Port Blair city. Though there is no specific area/village/*Basti* was developed with Muslim families during British period. But main pockets are South Point, Aberdeen Bazar, Phonix Bay, Shadipur, where their numbers more in compared to other areas.

The Moplah Muslims were basically settled by British on land in rural areas of South Andaman. After completing their imprisonment/conviction period, all Moplahs were retained in Andaman with agricultural land. They were settled in Bambooflat, Manarghat, Stewardjung, Calicut, Wimberligunj. Apart from that, a good number of Moplah families have been settled in Port Blair city along with other settler families. A small number of families were shifted to Little Andaman along with agricultural land to avoid the overcrowding in South Andaman area.

However, long before the advent of British Government in Nicobar Islands, the Minicoyans from Laccadive Islands in Arabian Sea had settled down in Car Nicobar. The Minicoyans, who were Muslims, were reported to be the first to establish their business in Car Nicobar, while the Burmese were the first to introduce inter-caste marriage. Later, Muslim traders from Gujarat and Surat came into contact with Nicobari tribes. It is stated that Nicobari Muslims are the descendents of the Muslim traders who married girls belonging to indigenous tribes of the islands.

Occupation

During Penal Settlement period, all the convicted were allowed to settle in and around Port Blair and South Andaman and areas extended to Mayabunder, North Andaman. Accordingly, many *Basti* or Villages have come up by these families. Apart from Port Blair, many of the convicted families were allotted agriculture lands and hilly lands for plantation in South Andaman Villages.The Anniket and Cattlegunj in South Andaman developed by Bhantu families. The adults of these families were engaged in manual and hard works. They were employed in Forest, Revenue, PWD and Marine departments. British authorities engaged them to clean forest, construction of road and building.

Though, the Moplahs were basically settled in rural areas, and they had started cultivation of paddy and horticulture. As their basic root was in Kerala, hence they developed coconut &banana plantation both in plain and hilly areas. However, Port Blair city was developed as convicted families with many small villages or *basti*, few areas like Abredeen Bazar, Junglighat, Haddo became centre of commercial activities. Ration shop, grocery shop and hotels were set up to meet the demands of the local people. Few local families, Moplahs and Tamil had own petty business. As initially British head-quarter was in Ross Island, a small market complex was developed, with bakery items, clothes and ration etc. Among Muslim, Haji Farzan Ali Khan was a sound businessman and philanthropist. His properties were distributed for noble cause of charitable purposes.Latter period, few Gujarati Muslim families like M/s Akoojee Jedwet & Co. led the local business in Port Blair as well as Nicobar district. Apart from that during early independence period, many small business were managed by local Muslims and Moplahs, such as hotels, bakery and transport etc. popular hotels were Milan, Majesty, Bridge hotel, Kerala hotel, Bismillha hotel and bakery like Janta Bakery, Rahamatullha Bakery were famous in Port Blair. But people of the third generation were less interested in business.Most of the local people would prefer to join service under local administration. For last two decades, the fruits business in city areas is basically doing by Muslims from Bihar and Uttar Pradesh. Many hair cutting saloons are running by traditional barber community in Muslim community, who have come from Bihar.

Education : Past and Present

The education system during Penal Settlement was not advanced in islands. The English medium schools were opened for British children and children of Indian Officials. The children of ex-convicted were rarely get admission in those schools.These children and ordinary Indian families were basically availed education from Urdu medium schools run by local teachers. Nonetheless, a few children of that time were rarely persuaded higher education from Dhaka (Bangladesh) or Rangoon (Burma) University. Therefore, even children of second generation among old settlers could not resort proper education in these islands.The Moplahs, the Malayalee Muslim arrived in between 20's and 30's. The male convicts of Moplahs were mostly marginal farmers and poor tenants in Kerala. Mostly they were illiterate. The children of those families did not get proper educational facilities in their settlement areas, which was mostly available in Port Blair only.The modern free education to every islander is by Central Government, which is actually giving benefits to Muslim community along with other religious people of these islands. In every department under local administration, a good numbers of Muslims are employed in various categories of posts. The girl child among Muslim are more advance in modern education. A good number of girls are taking higher education in Islands as well as mainland institutions. Parents are so liberal to encourage their girl child to undergo various job oriented courses from professional institutions. Many of the girls among Muslim occupied top rank in Schools Boards from Islands.Ms. Shalia Shah, not only topper in Class XII Board but crack Indian Foreign

Service from Islands. In Open School, distance education from IGNOU and regular courses, the girls from Moplah community are found majority in number than boys.As a result a good percentage of Muslim women are also working in various capacities with all efforts. In Marine, Forest, Transports, Police, Tehsil departments, the presence of Muslims are considerable more in compared to other religions population.

Muslims in the Post-Independence

Post-Independence history of these islands is glorious in all respects.The Union Government had extended all types of facilities and scheme benefits through local administration for up-liftment of the socio-economic conditions of the post-settlers families. In the field of health, education, business, agriculture and transport, the best quality of services have been provided to local families.Hence, the Muslim people along with people from other religions have been living with great affinity, love and dignity. The bitter experience of partition followed by communal riots could not spoil the communal harmony and integrity of the island's society.

The Ex-convicted families built a society without discrimination of caste, community and religion. Though the British authority allowed the Indians to practice their own religion and culture. Therefore, separate Temples, Gurudawara and Mosque were built for different religion people. In spite of this difference, the social harmony was built among islanders.

The Union Government have extended uniform education system for all children.The multi-lingual education has been started, soon the population of a particular language group has been increased.Like mainland, no religion orientated education such as *Madrassa* or *Sanskrit Tol* system was introduced. Perhaps the single largest group among Muslim has been kept as age-old practice and tradition in their own society.Apparently, the islands Muslim can be divided into four category, according to their nature of origin, dress, habits, language, ritual and way of life. The Moplah – The

Malayalee *Kaka*, from Kerala (Malabar), the converted Nicobaree Tribes Muslim from Nicobar Group of Islands, Bengali Muslim from Bengal and rest from all provinces including Tamil Nadu. Apart from modern education, the local Muslim including Moplah have started their traditional Islamic basic courses for small children through Mosques and private institutions.The children of both sex attend this education, where some basic religion based knowledge is imparted in Arabic language, Hadish, Koran preaching is giving to them. Islamic Guidance Centre is pioneer in this field.The children are putting their habit with traditional dress and customs. Many more information are giving for up-liftment of the Muslim community. Poor and destitute children are receiving special care by these institutions. Hatim Khana is running to extend right help to orphans and poor children of this community. Like *Madrassa*, no separate pure Islamic/religion base institution has been recognised to give Muslim culture for the children of these islands.The centre is conducting seminar, multi-religion convention to interact with scholars of other religions.

In education, both the sexes are receiving equal and dignified treatment from family and community at large. It is not wrong to say that the Muslim girls are more advance in education and other job oriented training activities.In the higher education sector both professional and general, girls from Moplah community are more attentive than other religious communities. However, the Muslims of old settlers are well to do in all respects. Most of the families receiving good education provided by the administration free of cost.Moreover, the Ministry of Home Affairs have provided few reserve seats in Technical and Professional degree colleges in mainland for the meritorious students among islanders. Therefore, children of the local Muslim of both the sexes have been availing quota reservations in mainland colleges. The parents are not hesitated to send their girls for perusing higher education and join in Government and private jobs both in islands and mainland. As a result, many Muslim women became doctors, teachers, principals. Moreover, a good number of Muslim educated women have been working in various capacities in local administration.The Muslim community of these islands, who have been settled or migrated during British period recognised under Other Backward Class (OBC) along with other communities came before independence. The reservation in Government jobs in local administration under OBC category has given ample opportunity to avail good percentage of jobs. The presence of Muslims both male and female in Government department is more than 25 percent in various capacity.When, the rest of Indian Muslim have been victim of many odd situations in their respective areas, the island Muslims are all set free from any kind of prejudice and hindrance and enjoining equal status with other communities.We easily classify that Indian Muslims are minority and also socio-economically backward. However, the scholars like T H Chowdary denied the fact that the Post–Independence governing system is primarily responsible for making them underprivileged and backward. According to him "Backwardness" of Muslims in India compared to non-Muslims is self-invited. His valid arguments is family with larger members is responsible for their poverty. He said "is it ever possible for families with large number of children to quit poverty unless they take to modern education and acquire competition withstanding employable education and skills ?"(Chowdary, 2014)

The women of island Muslim have a special place in islands society. They are progressive and educated. Women are equally sharing the Government jobs with their male counterparts. They are in the high professional position and serving like doctors, engineers, principal, teachers and amalgamated staff in local administration. They are responsible citizens and representing in local body both in rural Panchayat and Urban Local Bodies. They enjoy more freedom and respects in their family and community lives. There is very rare incident of discrimination and social violence and "tripal talak" happened as it is happening in mainland society. In education, their presence is more than boys. Education through IGNOU or distance and open schools are concerned, the girls are more in number than boys.

Island's Muslim and Outside World

The families of Muslim community along with all members of ex-convicted of these islands had been followed an exiled life from their counterpart in mainland India during British regime. Time and again people with a convicted background, led an odd life and hesitated to interact with people coming from mainland.They were recognised by outsiders as descendants of convicted. Many of them, their forefathers came as prisoners, who committed heinous crimes and spent a life imprisonment. They looked down in front of outsiders.They hesitated to disclose their family background before strangers or non-islanders.Time has changes, now the attitude of the people coming from mainland are also changed. Now this *Kalapani* is called, the Land of Heroes, the land of sacrifies (Bhiroki Bhumi, Shahido–ki-Bhumi). But with the passage of time some kind of changes have been observed in the outlook of every community and religion.

In early sixties and seventies only selected students used to voyage in mainland for higher education. The education has changed the outlook of these families, when these children came back to these islands. A new relationship has been developed among educated local youths as well as their parents with mainland society. Gradually they are being accepting by other communities within island's society through frequent marital relations by violating religious barrier and compound. The local Muslim community also makes a unique change in their social life. Hence, very slowly, they have been respectfully recognised themselves with new status and respect both in island's as well as in mainland also. Their world of relationship has been developed across the sea boundary.The interaction with outsiders brought a positive change in the life of the local people and Muslim as such. Many of them are now proudly disclosed their ancestors life's history, the incidents that was happens with their forefathers.Everybody is happily accepting their recognition. Many of them have been trying to re-start a new relation with their relatives in mainland. The reunion among lost families has been started. However, meeting with other communities has brought a progressive and comprehensive changes in their socio-cultural lives. A new type of bond has been developed with other communities in all respects.

For a long time, the local community irrespective of their religious difference, they have been followed a liberal and mixed cultural life. The religion would never being made a criterion for separate identity. But time and again some kind of changes have been observed in the out-look of every community and religion. Hence, the remarks of Dr. S.N.H. Rizvi and Iar Ali Khan in their book about local Muslim may not be correct in that sense that it is found in very society that various religious movements initiated by people from mainland earmarked as turning point of the local from secular outlook to religious fanatism. This is particularly observed among the local Muslim population due to the impact of Tabliq –a movement by the Muslim to inseminate (seed) the fundamental preaching of Islam, which help them to get detached from the mainstream of the locals bending towards Sharia and Muslim personal law to guide their society and solve their problems and disputes according to Sharia (Rizvi and Khan, 2017, p. 97). But in due course, interaction with people from mainland and various provinces of the same religion, the sense of religion identity has made a great mark in their daily life activities. People of every religion wants their religion to become a perfect discipline of their respective culture and make it a habit and practice in their daily life cycle.The exposure of electronic media and is highlighting at all India level is making every one more conscious and perfect follower of their respective religion and customs. Man with religion perfectness in terms of dress, customs, rites or rituals is provoking every individual towards a community identity. Pakistan nuclear physicist, who has often fallen foul of the establishment, wrote in April 2018 "Education is a confusing term because it has a broad range of meanings. But at the extremes, lie two fundamentally different types –traditional education and modern education. Like oil and water, they do not mix. However, vigorously shaken. In traditional education knowledge comes by relation and is thus unchangeable; the content is fixed until eternity. Modern education, on the other hand, is 100 percent secular and this worldly. It shamelessly changes content according to need and circumstance, caring only about the here and now." (Ahmed, 2018)

In spite of such reality in life and culture, the communal harmony and integrity among all religions is the root of strength of island's culture. As because, after all, the people of these islands are uprooted from their land of origin. They wanted to become a true Indian by creating a sense of unity among all religions and faiths. In the multi-cultural society, the sense of acculturation is found in each other socio-cultural festival. All the major festivals and cultural activities find participation of Muslim community. Depavali, Holi, Dusehra festivals are celebrating by all communities.

Indian Vote bank politics and underprivileged of majority of Indian Muslim has caused many a division in the Indian Muslim society. However, the reality of Indian Muslims is that they have so many divisions based on reality of different schools of thoughts and also a diverse community.The Islam who invaded in India became accepted in medieval India as a caste group and not as a religious group. Mughals, Pathans, Turks, Sheikhs and Syeds were regarded as sub-castes. Whereas, the Indian who converted to Islam came to be conveniently regarded as outcastes. (Siddiqui : 2012, p. 8).

The converted Indian Muslim could not ignored their caste division. Though Indian Muslim Ulema refuse to accept the ground reality of Islam in India which is much hindered in caste politics as any other Indian religion. In Western Uttar Pradesh Muslim society, the strong caste system is still found reflected in the areas such as Jhojhas, Ranghars, Gharhas which are peculiar to Muslims of this area. The Muslims are divided along Hindu caste lines, i.e. Muslim Rajputs, Mode Jaat (Muslim Jat) and Khatri, Gujjar, Tyagi and Teli.On the other hand Ansaris, Qureshis, Rayans, Sulimanis and Saifis are as divided socially as any other caste groups. Above and all Shia-Sunni and Deobandi-Barelvi divides. All the divisions emerged based on different school of thoughts.Today, Muslims in rural India do not vote as a single religious group. Their caste rivalries are so strong that if, the Qurasehis vote for one party, the Ansari will vote for another. (*Ibid.,* 2012, p. 8).

The Congress party had a monopoly over the vote bank of Hindi belt for over more than four decades. However, the Mondalisation has changed the equation of Muslim votes and shared the vote bank from Congress camp by other parties. Now, Samajbadi Party and BSP, JD(U), RJD have divided the vote share of Muslim voters in their favour. So far as Islands Muslim society is concerned, the families of pre-independence (Local Born and Moplahs) are core supporters of Congress party. The Parliamentary elections started from 1967 in A and N Islands lone constituency, the supporters of Muslim in Port Blair city and rural South Andaman basically voted in favour of Congress candidate Mr. K R Ganeshan, first elected MP for two terms and Mr. M R Bhakta, consecutively for eight times. Muslim leaders like Mr. Abdulla Kutty from Moplah community (migrated from Kerala), who led the South Andaman rural Muslim and represented as Pradhan, Counselor of Pradesh Council for many years. Mr. A R Rahman was Congress President.Even the BJP has set up its organisational activity in early nineties, no Muslim leaders was found in islands politics.At primary level, Mr. Farooque Shekha like one or two young leaders joined BJP. Even today, the Congress has a strong hold over Muslim community in Andaman.

In Port Blair Municipal elections, Muslim leaders like Hamid Ali, M.A. Rahman and Mohd. Iqbal elected many times as ward Councilor. Even among Muslim, lady leaders like Rasheda Begum, Nabisa Begum, Firdosh Bibi, Jamila Bibi and Rubina Aziz (seating Ward councilor) represented city politics.Ms. Firdosh Bibi and Ms. Zubida Begum hold the post of Chairperson of Port Blair Municipal Council. Mr. O C Chakku was treasurer of Congress party for many years. Mr. Iqbal, Mr. Siddique holds the key post in Congress party. Mr. Ramzan Ali from Congress (Now in BJP), Abdul Rahman, TDP are active in city politics and represented as ward councilor. In rural local body politics, Ms.Mariayam Bibi an active and prominent Congress figure and became Zilla Adhyakshya for many terms.Mr. C Chakou was the founding president of Janta Dal (U) of A and N islands.Among Nicobare tribal community, Congress has had a strong hold. Mr. Ibrahim Ali Hussain was an influential tribal leader and hold the post of Vice-Chief Captain of Nicobar Tribal Council.

Ms. Aysha Mazeed from Nancowry island, group of Nicobar islands is prominent figure and core supporter of Congress party.

In the present volume we have included eleven research articles. The contributors are experts in their own subject field.These eleven articles have been distributed in four parts, namely

Part–One : Minorities and Sachar Committee Report.

Part–Two: Women Empowerment and Muslim Society.

Part–Three: Socio-Cultural Diversity and Islands Muslims.

Part–Four: Economy and Educational Perception in Islands Muslims.

In Part-One, we have included four articles entitled "Identity, Stereotypes and Sachar Committee Report; Muslims in India" by Professor Muzaffar Assadi. Second article by Dr. Palash C. Coomar and Ricklina Roychowdhury captioned "Demographic Transition of Indian Muslims with Special Reference to Andaman and Nicobar Islands". The third article by Dr. Ajitha Narendran and Dr. K. Rajmohan "A Study on Socio-Economic Status of Muslims in India". And the fourth article entitled as "Educational Advancement of Muslims: Post-Sachar Committee Scenario" by Dr. S. S. Sreekumar.

In Part-Two we have incorporated three articles–one by Mrs. Swati Chakroborty "Right to Education :A Status of Muslims Women of India – Broken Promises". The second article of Part-Two, Women Empowerment and Muslim Society entitled "State, Religion and the Issues of Empowerment –The Status of Muslim Women in India" by Prof. K.M. Sajad Ibrahim. The third article of Part-Two by Dr. Anita Bannerjee captioned as "Muslim Women in the Context of Sachar Committee Report: A Reference to Mayabunder Tahsil of North Andaman".

In Part-Three we have included three research articles–the first one is by Dr. Hema Bannerjee entitled "Marriage, Society and Cultural Diversity among Island's Muslims". The next article of Part-Three by Dr. Kanwar Chanderdeep Singh entitled as "Making of Tradition : Perspectives on Hindu-Muslim Relations in Andaman and Nicobar Islands". The third article on "Growth of Muslim Society in Andaman and Nicobar Islands : A Historical Perspective" by Dr. T. Prasad Rao.

Only one article has been included in the Part-Four: Economy and Educational Perception in Island's Muslims by Dr. Sushim Kumar Biswas on "Socio-Economic Condition of Muslim Population in Andaman and Nicobar Islands: A Case Study of Immigrants from Bihar and West Bengal".

REFERENCES

Biswas, Swapan K. (2015), 'Interreligious Marriage in Nicobar Islands Opportunities and Challenges', *Economic and Political Weekly*, Vol. L, No. 22, May 30, 2015.

Chowdary, T.H. (2014), Muslim Backwardness, in *South Asian Politics*, Vol. 13(3), July.

Dhingra, Kinran (2005), *The Andaman and Nicobar Islands in the 20th Century: Gazetteer*, New Delhi, *A* Oxford University Press, 2007.

Justin, Anstice (1990), *The Nicobarese*, Calcutta, Seagull Book.

Khaled Ahmed (2018), Turning their back on modernity in *Indian Express*, 24/11/2018.

Ray, Pritin and Swapanesh Chaudhury (2012), *The Cost Horizon : A tale of Ross; The deserted Island;a Citadel*, Delhi, Farsight Publishers and Distributors.

SNH Rizvi and Iar Ali Khan (2017), *The Local Port Blair*: A bio-cultural profile. Delhi, B.R. Publishing Corporation.

Siddiqui, Shahid (2012), Believe me, Muslims are not a herd, *The Hindu*, 6/2/2012, p. 8.

Part-One
Minorities and Sachar Committee Report

2

Identity, Stereotypes and Sachar Committee Report: Muslims in India

Muzaffar Assadi

For the last couple of years there have been many debates as to whether Muslims in Indian context are facing deep identity crisis, given the fact that they constitute 15 percent of total population and also that there are 58 districts where the Muslim population constitute more than 25 percent. Secondly, the debates centred around the issues of development deficit and relative deprivation that they are undergoing. Finally the debate centred on the issue of security concerns of the community-will this community overcome from the deep feeling of "insecurity" and thereby comes out from "ghettoised life" can they participate in the political process as citizens? Or remain as single collective/homogeneous community?

All these issues came to surface after the submission of Sachar Committee report. Paradoxically, it took almost sixty years to undertake a comprehensive study on Muslims in India, as a minority group. Even though the debate on Muslims or Minorities in India dates back to the period of partition and subsequent Constituent Assembly debates. But Constituent Assembly debates centred around three important issues: one, to define who constitute Minorities, two, whether to extend reservation to Muslims and three, what are the rights that should be enshrined in Indian

Constitution to protect Minority rights. In the first case, although minorities were not defined in clear-cut terms, However, it was presumed to be religious and linguistic minorities. In this way Parsis, Sikhs, Christians, Muslims, Jains and Buddhists were treated as Minorities. Interestingly, Constitution clubbed Sikhs, Jains, and Buddhists as part of Hinduism, which was again reaffirmed in Hindu Marriage Act also. But in all the practical sense – particularly in Census reports, Committee reports such as Ranghanath Mishra Commission report-Sikhs, Jains, Buddhists were treated separately as "different religion" and Minorities. This is where the paradox lies. Nonetheless, in the political discourses and academic discourses Muslims are largely treated as Minorities in India.

There are two domains of rights that are available to Minorities in India. One is the common domain where the rights available to other citizens are also available to Muslims – such as right to equality, right to freedom, right against exploitation etc. On the contrary we have separate domain-rights specific to Minorities to protect their culture, conserve their distinct language, script, provision to establish educational institute and impart education, wearing and carrying their traditional symbols (such as Kripan by Sikh).

In the third case the constituent assembly did not approve extending reservation to Minorities particularly Muslims. There was hardly any dissenting voice. Even Maulana Azad, a votary of Minorities in Congress did not speak on the motion. In fact, the issue of reservation remained one of the major issues in post-independence India. The first Backward Class Commission completely ruled out reservation to Minorities as Kaka Kallekar thought the religion does not permit to carry the historical baggage of caste practice into Islam. Mandal Commission did speak of 'caste like structure including Hindu *Biradari* system among Muslims.

Even the attempts made at the regional level to introduce inclusive policies did not help the Muslims much. In Karnataka, for example, was introduced affirmative action along with Kolhapur state long back in 1920s. In Bihar we had Mungerilal Committee etc. Despite all these committee reports Muslims remained socially and economically backward. They faced development deficit as well as relative deprivation vis-à-vis others.

Paradoxically, globalisation further pushed them to marginality. The economics of globalisation displaced thousands of Muslims from their traditional work and skills. The increasing communalisation, global incidents of September 11, Bombay attack etc. created multiple crises. It was in this context the Indian State took upon itself to understand the socio-economic status of Muslims in India.

Crisis, Stereotypes

It is true that Muslims in India are in deep identity crisis. They carry the burden of partition which has led to sieze mentality. The fact that they are the part of larger universal *Ummah,* any happening taking place elsewhere at the global level also has castigating effect on them. The growing communalism and communal divide, the terrorist attacks, increasing violence, ghettoisation of the community etc. has further sharpened the identity crisis.This has led to stereotyping of the community as "anti-national", "radicals" terrorist, etc. They carry the double burden of being labelled as "anti-national "and as "being appeased" at the same time.

In the midst, of this very presence of a "Muslim identity" itself has created many myths and stereotypes. One of the perpetual myths that has been constructed is the fact that Muslims in Indian context speak only one language and that Urdu has become the symbol of their identity. Urdu is the language of South Asia. However, it is a half truth that it is the language exclusively spoken by the Muslims. In fact, Urdu evolved over the years out of the interaction between different dialects in India and represented the Hindu-Muslim exchange for many centuries. Although in the contemporary period Urdu is largely seen as "cultural product" (Raza Rumi, 2012) of Muslims and that of the linguist movement that went into the making of pure Urdu. However, Urdu is not declared as the mother tongue of large number of Muslims. Incidentally less than half of Indian Muslims declare Urdu as their mother tongue. In states such as Uttar Pradesh only 41.5 percent have recorded Urdu as their mother tongue. In fact, Urdu is a predominant language of Muslims in UP, Karnataka, Tamil Nadu, Uttar Pradesh, Bihar, Maharashtra, Rajasthan and Madhya Pradesh than in other states (Ahmed, 2006). Nonetheless there are communities among the Muslims declaring Navayati, Bengali, Malayalam, Bairy language as mother tongue instead of Urdu. Incidentally the state also has treated Urdu as the symbol of Muslim identity. This is the reason why it is promoting Urdu, supporting the Urdu schools etc. This has once again translated into stereotyping of Muslims as being appeased community.

Other myth that has been perpetuated over the years is that Muslims are a homogeneous community, who are averse to differentiate themselves from different ethnicity, language, region, including the fact that they never believe in such social structure as caste. But different studies have proved that caste did exist among Muslims. Satish Deshpande and Geetika Bapna in their seminal work has suggested that the Dalit Muslim is fact.They also have become the victim of same social discrimination, social distancing, social differences (Satish Deshpande and Geetika Bapna). Such arguments are quite apparent in the work of Imtiyaz Ahmed and others. Even the courts invariably have recognised the presence of castes among Muslims. Judgment of Ratnavel Pandian J. is very much relevant here:

> *"As far as Islam is concerned, Islam also does recognise castes or caste system. However, among the Muslims, in fact there are Ashrafs and Ajlafs, i.e., high born and low born.... All other Mohamedans including the occupational groups and all converts of lower ranks are known by the contemptuous terms, Ajlafs, wretches or 'mean people'....In some places a third class, called 'Arzal' or lowest of all is added. With them no other Mohamedan would associate and they are forbidden to enter the mosque and to use the public burial ground. Within these groups, there are castes with social precedence of. Exactly the same nature as one finds*

> *among the Hindus...., At present there are many social groups among Muslims which are included in the list of Scheduled Castes in some states. This shows that the Muslims in India have not remained immune from the same social evils as are prevalent among the Hindus."*[1] (Shaheen *et. al.*, 1994)

At all India level the castes among Muslims were identified long back in 1935 when British Government identified backward or Dalit Muslims then. This went on until the inauguration of the Republic. However, Ambedkar was one who identified Dalit-Muslims who are actually converted from Dalit community. This argument was implicitly accepted by Backward Class Commissions particularly Mandal as well as Havanoor Commission in Karnataka in 1970s when it identified different categories among the Muslims. For example, Halalkore, Laddaf, Pinjari. Incidentally these categories comes from Backward caste. In fact, Mandal Commission had earlier identified "caste like social structure existing" among Muslims. This is further strengthened by Sachar Committee report and Ranganath Committee Report in recent years. They have identified three kinds of castes prevailing among Muslims: Ashrafs, Arjals and Arzals. The first belonged to upper caste, second largely middle caste and the last one to Dalits castes, In fact, these categories follow values of castes although Islam doesn't recognise the presence of caste among the Muslims. In Islam caste is known as *Zaat*, the same is often used in popular usage in India. Hence it is true that caste or *Zaat* is not an exclusive domain of Hindus, this is mainly because majority of Muslims in India are local converts. However, question remains as to whether caste would become the defining point of social relations among the Muslims. The recent debate as well demand for 4.5 percent reservation from within the Dalit reservation for the Dalit –Muslims has brought sharp reaction from Dalit fronts. However, it is true that caste would become a defining point in the years to come when caste is recognised by the political system as a social reality.

Reports and Attempts at Minority Welfare

One myth is again and again produced to state that the Sachar Committee was the first Committee constituted to study the socio-economic conditions of Muslims in India. Incidentally prior to Sachar Committee report there were attempts at the central as well as the state level to focus on them-neither they were comprehensive one nor were they focussed study on Muslims.

One of the first Panels to be appointed was Gopal Singh Panel in 1980 to study the socio-economic conditions including Minorities, SCs, STs and Other Weaker Social categories. It submitted its report in 1983, however, its recommendations and the findings were not discussed until late 1980s. It clearly identified the "sense of discrimination among the minorities" and called for addressing such decimation so as to bring them into the mainstream.

It was during the same time the Government of India came out with fifteen point programme to address the issues of Minorities-the fifteen point programme was initially initiated by the then Prime Minister Mrs Indira Gandhi in 1983 and followed by Rajiv Gandhi in 1985 in their letter to the Chief Ministers. The major recommendations in the fifteen point programmes include the following:

1. Dealing the issues of communal conflict with highest degree of impartiality
2. Awarding those who have done good work
3. Severe action against those who incite and participate in communal riots
4. Establishment of special courts to deal with the issues of communal offences and speedy trials
5. Immediate relief to those who are affected by communal riots and adequate financial assistance for their rehabilitation.
6. Usage of media to build and restore confidence among people
7. Pressurising the media to be impartial as well as avoiding the publication of sensitive issues which would incite communal riots

8. Giving priority to Minorities in the appointment of police personnel
9. Similar priority in the recruitment of central government police personnel
10. Stress on the appointment of Minorities in public sectors and key sectors such as police,

Similar exercise was done at regional level too. In Karnataka, for example, the Minority Commission headed by Rehman Khan in 1998 came out with the report which reinforced the argument of development deficit and deprivation among the Muslims.

Sachar Committee and the Concerns of the Community

Government of India in 2005 appointed High Level Committee under Rajender Sachar to study the "Social, Economic and Educational status of the Muslim Community in India". Its report is hailed as "first of its kind to understand the backwardness". At the outset the Committee Report focused on three important concern of the community. One, Identity related concerns two, security related concerns and three, equity related concerns.

(a) Identity Related Concerns: In this context Sachar Committee discussed three important inter-related issues visibility in public spaces, housing and education and gender and identity. It is argued that the visibility in the public space as being Muslim has become problematic for many the symbols of *Burqa, Purdha, Topi* and beard-have become cause for concern for majority of them.This has become point of exclusion too *hijab* wearing Muslim women were finding it increasingly difficult to find jobs. Muslim women in *hijab* complain of impolite treatment in the market, hospitals, in schools, in accessing public facilities such as public transport (High Level Committee Report, 2006).

It is argued further that the Muslim identity affects every day life practices it ranges from being unable to rent/buy a house to accessing good schools for their children. Buying or renting property in localities of one's own choice is becoming increasingly difficult for Muslims. Apart from the reluctance of owners to rent or sell property to Muslims, several housing societies in non-Muslim localities dissuade Muslims from locating them (*Ibid.*, 2006).

Thirdly, Muslim identity is also constructed in terms of gender discrimination, gender – injustice in the community. This has created a stereotyping about the community: that the community is reluctant to extend freedom, autonomy to women. Incidentally Sachar Committee argues that, "for large number of Muslim women in India today, the only safe space in terms of physical protection and in terms of protection of identity is within the boundaries of home and community. Everything beyond the walls of the ghettos is seen as unsafe ad hostile-markets, roads, lanes and public transport, schools and hospitals, police stations and government offices"(Sachar, 2006).

(b) Security Related Concerns: Muslims are increasingly feeling insecure in the context of communal riots. Even the role played by the state agencies including the police and bureaucracy has accentuated feeling of "insecurity" among the Muslims. This has multiplied the growth of "ghettos" for living and for security. At the same time this migration from non-Muslim locality to Muslim locality has adversely affected the economy of Muslims-they have pushed to marginality again and again.

(c) Equity Concerns: It is argued that sense of alienation and sense of discrimination among the Muslims is very high.This is perpetuated due to the fact that Muslim localities are lacking in civic amenities, inadequate representation in politics, inadequacy in power sharing, inadequate representation in bureaucracy, low levels of education, increasing poverty among the Muslims, poor access to schools, communal content of the school text, low enrolment and retention of women in school etc have caused a sense of discrimination among the Muslims. This is called for reworking on the issues of "social equity" vis-à-vis the others.

Its arguments are based on three principles: One, principle of demystifying some stereotypes, two, argument of relative deprivation and development deficit that the community is facing. And three, principle of identifying the areas of intervention so as to address the relevant issues.

Stereotypes and Sachar Committee

It is true that Sachar Committee report also demystified some of the stereotypes about Muslims:

One, other than the presence of three castes-Ashrafs, Ajlafs, Arzals, -among Muslims, the Committee for the first time identified the presence of various OBCs who have the common *Biradaris*. While identifying the OBCs the committee argued that, 'hierarchical ordering of social groups, endogamy and hereditary occupation has been found to amply present among the Indian Muslims as well". Sachar Committee identified two broad categories as belonged to OBC categories of Muslims: (a) Those who are equivalent to Hindu OBCs the Ajlafs (b) Those equivalent to Hindu SCs, the Arzals. In both the cases it identified such caste as Halalkores, Helas, Ibegis or Bhangis, Dhobis, Nais, Hajjams, Chiks, Faquirs, Juhalas, Darzi, Idiris, Kunjaras, etc as the one belonged to OBCs–both Hindu OBCs and Muslim OBCs have common ancestry. They constitute 40.7 percent of Muslim population.

Further, this report exposed the inbuilt stereotypes of the institutions vis-à-vis the Muslims. This is apparent in the way the Banking sector has failed to reach out to Muslim dominant areas as service provider. Sachar Committee has argued that access to Banking sector is low and inadequate including the fact that the average credit disbursed to the community is also meager. This is not simply restricted to public sector banks alone, but also other financial institutions such as SDBI, NIRD too. On the one hand non-accessibility in the rural side is due to absence of adequate banks in the Muslim dominated villages and secondly it is also due to inherent bias of the banking sector too. This is apparent when they identified the Muslims predominant areas as "negative zones", "red lining areas" or "red zones".

Thirdly, the stereotype is about the growth rate. There has been a consistent argument that Muslim growth rate is higher when compared to other, particularly Hindus. It argued that, the recent inter Census decade 1991-2001, has shown a decline in the growth rate of Muslims in most of the States.

Further the stereotype is centring on the issue of sending children to *Madrassa* schools. Muslims as a social category would send more number of children to *Madrassa* education/schools as the *Madrassa* have been treated and seen as institutions "encouraging religious fundamentalism and creates a sense of alienation". On the contrary Sachar Committee argues that the number of Muslims attending *Madrassa* education is far less than the one believed.-only three percent of the children of school going age at all India level are enrolled in the *Madrassa* education/institution. This misconception is the result of misunderstanding between *Madrassas* (religious schools) and *Muktabas* (part time religious schools).

Further, it demystified the argument that every Muslim child attend the Urdu medium school, as Urdu is treated as mother tongue of Muslims. On the contrary the Sachar Committee argues that, barring Karnataka, Maharashtra and Andhra Pradesh the children enrolled in other states in Urdu medium are dismally low. This is apparent in the case of Uttar Pradesh, Jharkhand and Bihar. Incidentally the lack of adequate Urdu schools and facilities in the Muslim predominant areas has had its effects on the performance of children-their performance is treated as very "poor" by any standard and thereby they become excluded in the employment market.

Further, the stereotype centred on the issue of modern education-it is said Muslims are averse to modern education. On the contrary, Sachar Committee argues that, "Muslim parents are not averse to modern or mainstream education and to sending children to the affordable Government schools" (Sachar, 2006, p. 85).

Another perception is about girl education. There is a strong perception or stereotype that Muslims do not prefer girl child to be educated. On the contrary, it is argued that girl children are enrolled; they are enrolled both in Government schools as well as non-Government schools. The argument of withdrawal of girl child from the school literally linked to the issues of "non-availability of schools" within easy reach for girls at lower level of education, absence of girl hostels, absence of female teachers and availability of scholarships as they move up the education (Sachar, 2006, p. 85).

Deprivation and Development Deficit

Sachar Committee argued that Muslims are doubly marginalised: one side they are relatively deprived vis-a-vis other Hindus or general population; secondly they are increasingly marginalised due to development deficit. Their deficit is no different from other deprived communities such as Dalits, sometime it is worse than Dalit categories.

a. Education and Literacy

It starts with education and literacy rate.The literacy rate among the Muslims is just 59.1 percent which is below the national average of 65 percent. Sachar Committee reported as many as 25 percent of children of age group of 6-14 either not attending the schools or dropped out from the schools. The number of illiterate children is also quite high among the general Muslims it is 33.3 percent. Only 17 percent of Muslim children have done matriculations. This number gets further skewed when they move to the upper level of education. At the graduate level their number comes down to 3.6 percent and the number of technically qualified is just 0.4 percent. In terms of the participation in the specific institution such as IIMs and IITs they form 1.3 percent, 1.7 percent (graduate level) respectively. With regard to medical education their representation slightly better but still it is inadequate-4 percent.This is the same in the case of enrolment in general stream courses as well as science courses. "The share of the Muslims in all courses is low at the PG level and marginal in the science stream" (Sachar, 2006). Interestingly Committee report again dismissed the argument that majority of Muslims send their children to *Madrassas* only 3 percent go to *Madrassas* and 66 percent attend government schools. In fact, Muslim children are relatively deprived off when compared to the children of other communities. Many a time they are worse off than the Dalits.

Table 2.1

Socio-religious Communities	Number (in Lakhs)	Percentage of 20 years plus	Distribution Across the Communities (SRCs)
Total	Graduates, Diploma and Certificate	Graduate, Diploma and certificates	Graduates, Diploma and Certificates
Total	376.7 (40.5)	6.7 (0.7)	100 (100)
Muslim	23.9 (2.7)	3.6 (0.4)	6.3 (6.8)
SCs/STs	30.8 (4.1)	2.4 (0.3)	8.2(10.2)
All others	322 (33.7)	8.8 (0.9)	85.5 (83.0)

Source : Sachar Committee Report, 2006.

(b) Poverty and Job Market

The Committee argues that the incident of poverty is highest among Muslims-it is 35 percent among the general Muslims and 38 percent among Muslim OBCs. Job market is one space where the deprivation is glaring. Even though they constitute nearly 15.4 percent of total population, their representation in the job market is just 6.4 percent, whereas in the case of SCs /STs their participation in the salaried job market is extremely low. This is true in the case of their participation in the urban formal job market-they constitute less than eight percent of workers in the urban areas. Large number of Muslim regular workers are on piece-rates system, fewer Muslims get regular salaries. Even the average wages that they get is less than that of the "Hindus".They do not constitute big chunk of population in agriculture less than 40 percent are engaged in agriculture as agricultural workers.

Even Public Sector undertaking is no different. Their representation in public sector is almost negligible. Committee argues that, in general Muslims are in inferior jobs such as clerical or class IV employees compared to Hindus. The share of the Muslims at the higher level, managerial level just 2.3 percent and 2.8 percent at the middle level. Their representation in the Security/Police and

Defence related activities shows once again the dismal picture. In the former case they are just about six percent when compared to Hindus who represent 42 percent. In the case of Defence they constitute only four percent when Hindus represents more than 33 percent.

(c) Government Employment and Programmes

This sector is once again disappointing. In the state level departments their representation remains at 6.3 percent. In railways they constitute only 4.5 percent, in Banks and RBI they constitute 2.2 percent; in security agencies such as Border Security Force, Central Reserve Police Force, Central Industrial Security Force and Sahastra Seema Bal Muslim represent 3.2 percent ; in postal services they constitute 5.0 percent and finally, in the University they represent only 4.7 percent.

In the Central Government department the share of Muslims increases marginally for lower level jobs. However, in group D the share of Muslims is just five percent. This is even less in the Public sector under takings. In the public sector banks their participation is 2.2 percent. Similarly, in the case of Central civil service, Muslims are found to be only 3 percent in IAS, 1.8 percent in the IFS, and four percent in IPS.

Strange but true, that some of the states which boasted of transformative politics have made little efforts to accommodate Muslims in the state Government structures. In West Bengal only 4.7 percent of Muslims are found in higher position when the total population of Muslims is around 25 percent. In the same state 1.8 percent are found in lower level jobs. Kerala and Assam are the two states where the positions are slightly better-10.3 and 10.2 percent respectively in higher position. In state like Uttar Pradesh they constitute 7.5 and 4.9 percent respectively. There is a mismatch between the state population and the employment in the Government sector.

(d) Industry and Other Sectors

If one looks industry-wise, the same trend of deprivation is visible. In agriculture, livestock and forestry, their percentage is 39.1 percent which is less compared to Hindus(58.9 percent), in mining and quarrying industry it is just 0.3 percent. In electricity, gas and water it is just 0.3 percent, construction it is 6.8 percent, finance and in insurance it is again 1.2 percent. In all these cases Muslims are a deprived lot.

The deprivation is also visible in the case of banking sector. Only 12 percent of the total could to open their account, but strangely the report exploded one more myth: that Muslims constitute the large number of defaulters. In fact, Sachar Committee argues that only 4.6 percent of the total population have outstanding loans to the Public Sector undertaking banks.

(e) Access to Social and Physical Infrastructure

This is also true even in the case of access to social and physical infrastructure. It is argued that Muslim populated areas lack basic facilities such as schools, roads, medical facilities, sanitation etc. Its findings are glaring both in rural villages and urban areas:

- More than 1000 Muslim concentrated villages in West Bengal, and Bihar do not have any educational facilities,
- Almost 2000 Muslim concentrated villages in Assam and Jammu and Kashmir, more than 3000 villages in West Bengal and Bihar, more than 5000 villages in Uttar Pradesh are without any medical facilities.
- Same situation exist in the case of access to Post and Telegraph in Muslim concentrated states in West Bengal, Jammu and Kashmir, Assam and Bihar.
- The proportion of *pacca* roads is lower in the same states.
- Their houses are less electrified compared to those of other Hindus in Muslim concentrated villages. "The share of villages with no electricity ceases with increase in the Muslim population".

- In the Muslim concentrated villages they have least access to tap water.
- More than sixty percent of the rural populations do not have the access to modern or clean fuel such as LPG, Electricity including Kerosene.
- Muslim inhabiting areas lack better roads, drainage, and sewage water supply.

(f) Poverty Consumption and Standard of Living

Even here too the deprivation is very well established. On the issue of means Per Capita Expenditure, Sachar Committee argues that, in urban areas in almost all the states the Mean Per Capita Expenditure is substantially low when compared to that of other Hindus, -but incidentally they are better in the rural areas.

- Inequality in consumption is higher in urban areas than in the rural areas.
- Muslims own very meager percentage of land compared to Hindu generals, including the fact that the average land size and holding that they hold is less.
- Incidence and intensity of poverty among the Muslims in urban areas, such as in smaller towns, is highest. Nearly 40 percent Muslims fall under poorest monthly per capita expenditure class. Similar trend is discernible in villages in many states.

(g) Access to Government Programmes

It is true that 38 percent of Muslims in urban areas and 27 percent in rural areas live below the poverty line. This has denied them bank loans, or credits from the Government institutions. This is the reason why Government programmes become critical to this community. In fact, state-wise analysis is done by the Committee shows the poor access to different Government schemes. In Kerala, their share under various programmes ranges between five percent and 18 percent, in Uttar Pradesh it ranges between three and 14 percent. Few states such as Maharashtra, Karnataka have shown satisfactory results in some cases. In other schemes such as Integrated Child Development Schemes barring these three states, other states have shown a dismal picture Bihar 1.7 percent, Uttar Pradesh 1.9 percent respectively.

(h) Politics of Representation and Deficit

Muslims not only face development deficit but also deficit of representation in politics. Couple of things has gone against them: delimitation of constitutions, lack of political leadership etc. Muslim representation is inadequate both in the case of Parliament as well as other structures of Parliamentary Democracy. Muslim dominated constituencies' have been converted into reserved constituencies.

All these make us ask the question: where are the Muslims. They are largely found in home based work and street vending, rag picking, cycle vending, or they are found in self-employed activities followed by casual labour they are much larger in number in informal sector they constitute 92.6 percent (male). In fact, their representation is relatively higher in manufacture of tobacco products, manufacture of textiles and textile products such as wearing apparel. In manufacture of fabricated metal products, land transport and retail trade, they are found in significant number in sale, repair, and maintenance of motor vehicles, some segment of electrical machinery their number is considerable.They are more in number in the case of sales persons, tailors, dress makers, transport equipment operators, spinners, weavers, knitters machinery fitters, assemblers and precision instrument makers, carpentry related works and blink laying/construction work. All these prove that a community despite affirmative action and different policy measures was not able to come up economically as well as politically. This has created deep sense of alienation as well as frustration among the Minorities. Meanwhile one cannot deny the fact that the community is now in deep identity crisis. This is the reason why the Sachar Committee came out with series of interventions in terms of the public policies. These interventions are as follows:

(a) Intervention is sought in the area of education, skill development, and flow of credit where Muslim workers are found in good number.

(b) Intervention sought to augment better infrastructure facilities in Muslim dominated areas-both in villages and urban areas.

(c) Intervention is sought in the case of alleviating Muslims at the poverty level.

(d) Intervention is sought to sensitise the bureaucracy about the programmes available to the minorities/ Muslims.

(e) Intervention is also sought to give representation to Muslims in the selection panels.

(f) Intervention is sought to increase the Muslim participation in the public policy making.

Recommendations

Sachar Committee came out with series of recommendations-one is general policy recommendations and another is specific policy recommendation. Some of the policy measures include the following:

- Creation of a National Data Bank.
- Legal provisions to provide equal opportunities.
- Enhancing the participation in governance.
- Formulating and implementing new nomination procedure for better representation.
- Establishing more rational procedure for delimitation of constituencies.
- Establishment of Equal Opportunity Commission.
- Establishing linkage between diversity and incentives-institutions having high volume of diversity is given more incentives than the less one.
- Facilitating the creation of more common public spaces.
- Setting up of high quality government schools.
- Developing a Diversity Index (DI) in respect of institutions in order to mainstream the minorities and induce greater diversity.

Will it bring in paradigm shift in the lives of Muslims in India? One thing is fairly clear that the studies conducted after the submission of Sachar Committee report have reconfirmed the findings of Sachar. Seven surveys commissioned by the Maharashtra State Minority Commission in recent past(2011) demonstrated that the Muslims live in dismal conditions-nearly 32.4 percent Muslims reported themselves as "workers" and nearly 70.7 percent engaged in category of work activities such as semi-skilled and skilled informal sector work such as carpentry, masonry, electrician, plumber, mechanic, manual labour, coolie job, solid waste management, butchery, weaving, beadwork, *jari* and embroidery work, tailoring, hawking, petty trade, pulling cycle rickshaws and handcarts, driving four wheelers and heavy vehicles. Adding to this report Muslims suffer from institutional bias. Banks for example refuse to disburse loans to Muslims-the amount of loan disbursed to Muslim is far less than what the other Minorities such as Buddhists and Sikhs. Further their backwardness is also linked to larger inadequacy in the representation – both in politics and in bureaucracy(it is just one percent for the last three decades in the case of IAS and IPS cadre of Maharashtra). Incidentally the findings located the reason for the socio-economic backwardness in the increasing communal riots and the subsequent civic rupture due to ghettoisation of the community. In fact, Maharashtra is one of the states wherein communal riots have become recurring phenomenon-between 1998 and 2008 Maharashtra had witnessed 1,192 communal clashes (Government of Maharashtra, 2013). Every communal riot has pushed them to become part of ghettos and marginality. Such findings are reaffirmed by another commission: Ranganath Mishra Commission. The latter has advanced reservation for Dalit-Muslims within the Dalit quota. This has led to serious debate with regard to identifying Dalit Muslims category within Muslim and also providing "religion based reservation".

It was during this time that the Indian state came out with 15 point programme which included the following:

1. Equitable availability of the Integrated Child Development Services (ICDS). Under this programme it became incumbent

to-provide services such as better supplementary nutrition, immunisation, and health check-up and free education.

2. Improving access to School Education particularly establishing Sarva Shishka Abhiyan, Kasturba Gandhi Balika Vidyalaya scheme and other similar schemes in villages/ localities wherein minority population lives
3. More resources for teaching Urdu including Assistance in recruitment and posting of Urdu language teachers in primary and upper primary schools.
4. Modernising *Madarsa* Education.
5. Scholarships for meritorious students from minority communities.
6. Improving educational infrastructure through the Maulana Azad Education Foundation.
7. Self-Employment and Wage Employment for the poor.
8. Upgradation and Opening new ITIs in areas predominantly inhabited by minority communities.
9. Enhanced credit support for economic activities.
10. Recruitment to State and Central Services particularly in police, railways, banking sector is given to minority candidates.
11. Equitable share in rural housing scheme.
12. Implement Integrated Housing and Slum Development Programme and Jawaharlal Nehru National Urban Renewal Mission in minority populated regions of slum areas.
13. Prevention of communal incidents.
14. Prosecution for communal offences.
15. Rehabilitation of victims of communal riots. (Prime Minister's New 15 points programmes).

Three more schemes were added in the year 2009 to this 15 point programme

1. National Rural Drinking Water Programme (NRDWP)

2. Urban Infrastructure Development Scheme for Small and Medium Towns (UIDSSMT).

Despite, all these policy measures and recommendations, the conditions of Muslims have not improved much. They still revolve around twin deprivations: development deficit as well as relative deprivation. This is very much obvious in various reports. The approach paper to the XII Five Year Plan states that there is a serious problem as the enrolment and GER for the Muslim population is much lower than that for non-Muslim students.

Similarly, the Standing Committee on Social Justice and Empowerment (Chairperson: Mr. Hemanand Biswal) which was appointed to oversee the implementation of Prime Ministers' 15 point programme pinpointed the fact that the literacy rate of Muslims be improved, access to scholarship be increased, employment opportunities be increased, develop more number of large and medium scale industries in Minority concentrated areas, CD block-wise programme involving various stakeholders should be evolved to address communalism etc. Even individual studies such as the one carried out by Abusaleh Shariff-January, 2013 have proved the obvious : the prevalence of huge gap between Muslims and others Muslims still lag in accessibility. The sense of deprivation is very high. Even the "latest data on development outcomes (Government of India, 2011; NSSO, 2011; NSSO 2013) do not show any significant improvements in the conditions of Muslims" (Hussain, 2014).

Will Muslims overcome from the deep identity crisis, crisis of equity and security in the midst of policy measures, and development paradigms a question in the years to come remains questions. In fact, the increasing intervention to bring in a paradigm shift among the Muslims one the one hand, the continued development deficit and relative deprivation on the other will remain the hall mark of politics in the years to come. Here lies the paradox of development too.

REFERENCES

Raza Rumi (2012), Myths about the Urdu language, *The Express Tribune*, February, 4, 2012.

Maqbool Ahmed Siraj (2006), Urdu and Muslims, *Islamic Voice*, Nov. 2006.

Despande, Satish and Geetika Bapna (2008), *Dalit in the Muslim and Christian Communities : A Status Report on Current Social Scientific Knowledge* (Prepared for the National Commission for Minorities, GOI, University of Delhi, Delhi, 2014.

Rafia Shaheen (1994), *Miss Rafia Shaheen And Etc. Vs. State of Karnataka And Others* on March, 1994.

Sachar Committee Report (2006), *High Level Committee Report on Socio-economic and Educational Status of the Muslim community of India*. Nov. 2006.

Department of Economics (2013), *SNDT Women's University*, Mumbai, Commissioned by Maharashtra State Minority Commission, Govt. of Maharashtra, Socio-Economic Profile of Muslims: A State Profile of Maharashtra.

Prime Minister's New 15 Point Programmes for the Welfare of Minorities. http:// social justice.nic.in/pdf/anne 13pm 15p.pdf.

Sajad Hussain, *Muslim Inclusion in India : A Review of Literature,* http://centreforequalitystudies.org/wp content /uploads/2014/01/ WP004_Review of Literature-on-Muslims-exclusion_Sajid –Hussain.

3

Demographic Transition of Indian Muslim with Special Reference to Andaman and Nicobar Islands

Palash C. Coomar and Ricklina Roychowdhury

The Muslim is a universal community and their religion is also a universal one. In the present day Muslims are found in almost all the countries of the world. "They are all united by the bond of common religion and believe in the same basic tenets of Islam, which are *Imam*, *Namaz*, *Roza*, *Sakat* and *Hoj* (faith, prayer, fasts, tithes or tax and pilgrimage to Mecca) and the religious code." (Rahman, 2000, p.513). Though all the Muslims all over the world follow all these, still Muslims living in different parts of the world have much difference amongst them. The reason behind these differences in the culture and way of living is that they belong to different societies and have distinct culture.

Mujeeb in connection with the Indian Muslims states – "The structure of Indian Muslim society has had little resemblance to the demographic, classless community, integrated and inspired by belief in the one God which the Indian Muslim fondly imagines it to have been" (Mujeeb, 1972, p. 81).

According to Shakir, during coming of Muslims in India, Islam was no longer in the original form as it had undergone significant changes due to accumulation of wealth and contact with other cultures and so on (Shakir, 1970, p. 24).

Islam has always encouraged Muslims to become good human beings. The Holy Quran "exhorts Muslims to be kind, generous, just and truthful in all their dealings with other men, not just Muslims: (Rahman, 2000, p. 514). A true Muslim must always be just and truthful even if for this he/she suffers from a loss of his/her relatives or even it benefits an enemy." There is a famous *Hadith* (saying of the Prophet) which states that "he is not a good Muslim whose neighbour remains hungry while he is well fed."

The Muslims are free to adopt any local custom or trait if it does not interfere the basic tenets of Islam. "Muslim can adopt it and not feel guilty of un-Islamic because that custom is not practiced by Muslims ….." (Rahman, 2000, p. 514).

Before going inside the analyses please note the underneath points :

(a) Census was not conducted in Jammu and Kashmir during 1991 Census and in Assam in 1981 due to disturbed conditions.

(b) The 1991 figures for Uttaranchal-Uttar Pradesh, Jharkhand-Bihar, Chhattisgarh-Madhya Pradesh have been recasted as per the jurisdiction in 2001 Census.

(c) Andaman &Nicobar Islands, Chandigarh, Dadra and Nagar Haveli, Daman and Die, Delhi, Lakshadweep and Pondicherry were Union Territories during 1991.

(d) Uttaranchal, Jharkhand and Chhattisgarh did not exist during 1991 Census. They were part of Uttar Pradesh, Bihar and Madhya Pradesh respectively.

Table 3.1 shows the distribution of General Population and Muslim Population with percentage of Total Population at India and States and Union Territories level of past three Censuses i.e. 1991, 2001 and 2011.

Table 3.1: India, States and Union Territories-wise Distribution of General and Muslim Population of Censuses 1991, 2001 and 2011

Country/States/Union Territories	Population			No. & Percentage of Muslim Population					
				1991		2001		2011	
	1991	2001	2011	No.	%	No.	%	No.	%
India	**846,421,039**	**1,028,737,436**	**1,210,854,977**	**101,596,057**	**12.12**	**138,188,240**	**13.43**	**172,245,158**	**14.23**
Jammu & Kashmir	NA	10,413,700	12,541,302	NA	—	6,793,240	65.23	8,567,485	68.31
Himachal Pradesh	5,170,877	6,077,900	6,864,602	89,137	1.70	119,512	1.97	149,881	2.18
Punjab	20,281,969	24,358,999	27,743,338	239,401	1.20	382,045	1.57	535,489	1.93
Chandigarh	642,015	900,635	1,055,450	17,477	2.70	35,548	3.95	51,447	4.87
Uttaranchal	7,050,634	8,489,349	10,086,292	NA	—	1,012,141	11.92	1,406,825	13.95
Haryana	16,463,648	21,144,564	25,351,462	763,775	4.60	1,222,916	5.78	1,781,342	7.03
Delhi	9,420,644	13,850,507	16,787,941	889,641	9.40	1,623,520	11.72	2,158,684	12.86
Rajasthan	44,005,990	56,507,188	68,548,437	3,525,339	8.00	4,788,227	8.47	6,215,377	9.07
Uttar Pradesh	132,061,753	166,197,921	199,812,341	24,109,684	17.30	30,740,158	18.50	38,483,967	19.26
Bihar	64,530,554	82,998,509	104,099,452	12,787,985	14.80	13,722,048	16.53	17,557,809	16.87
Sikkim	406,457	540,851	610,577	—	—	7,693	1.42	9,867	1.62
Arunachal Pradesh	864,558	1,097,968	1,383,727	—	—	20,675	1.88	27,045	1.95
Nagaland	1,209,545	1,990,036	1,978,502	20,642	1.70	35,005	1.76	48,963	2.47
Manipur	1,837,149	2,293,896	2,855,794	133,535	7.30	190,939	8.32	239,836	8.40
Mizoram	689,756	888,573	1,097,206	—	—	10,099	1.14	14,832	1.35
Tripura	2,757,205	3,199,203	3,673,917	196,495	7.10	254,422	7.95	316,042	8.60
Meghalaya	1,774,778	2,318,822	2,966,889	260,306	14.70	99,169	4.28	130,399	4.40
Assam	22,414,322	26,655,528	31,205,576	6,373,204	28.40	8,240,611	30.92	10,679,345	34.22
West Bengal	68,077,965	80,176,197	91,276,115	16,075,836	23.60	20,240,546	25.25	24,654,825	27.01

contd...

Jharkhand	21,843,911	26,945,829	32,988,134	NA	—	3,731,308	13.85	4,793,994	14.53
Odisha	31,659,736	36,804,660	41,974,218	577,775	1.80	761,985	2.07	911,670	2.17
Chhattisgarh	17,614,928	20,833,803	25,545,198	NA	—	409,615	1.97	514,998	2.02
Madhya Pradesh	48,566,242	60,348,023	72,626,809	3,282,800	5.00	3,841,449	6.37	4,774,695	6.57
Gujarat	41,309,582	50,671,017	60,439,692	3,606,920	8.70	4,592,854	9.06	5,846,761	9.67
Daman & Diu	101,586	158,204	243,247	9,048	8.90	12,281	7.76	19,277	7.92
Dadra & Nagar Haveli	138,477	220,490	343,709	3,341	2.40	6,524	2.96	12,922	3.76
Maharashtra	78,937,187	96,878,627	112,374,333	7,628,755	9.70	10,270,485	10.60	12,971,152	11.54
Andhra Pradesh	66,508,008	76,210,007	84,580,777	5,923,954	8.90	6,986,856	9.17	8,082,412	9.56
Karnataka	44,977,201	52,850,562	61,095,297	5,234,023	11.60	6,463,127	12.23	7,893,065	12.92
Goa	1,169,793	1,347,668	1,458,545	61,455	5.30	92,210	6.84	121,564	8.33
Lakshadweep	51,707	60,650	64,473	48,765	94.30	57,903	95.47	62,268	96.58
Kerala	29,098,518	31,841,374	33,406,061	6,788,364	23.30	7,863,842	24.70	8,873,472	26.56
Tamil Nadu	55,858,946	62,405,679	72,147,030	3,179,410	5.70	3,470,647	5.56	4,229,479	5.86
Pondicherry	807,785	974,345	1,247,953	52,867	6.50	59,358	6.09	75,556	6.05
Andaman & Nicobar Islands	280,661	356,152	380,581	21,354	7.60	29,265	8.22	32,413	8.52

It has been observed from Table 3.1 that at the National Level, percentage of Muslim population to total population during 1991, 2001 and 2011 Censuses are 12.12 percent, 13.43 percent and 14.23 percent respectively.

In 1991 Census, there were seven States/Union Territories where the percentage of Muslim population is higher than the National Average (12.12%). These States/Union Territories were Lakshadweep (94.30%), Assam (28.40%), West Bengal (23.60%), Kerala (23.30%), Uttar Pradesh (17.30%), Bihar (14.80%), and Meghalaya (14.70%).

In Andaman and Nicobar Islands the proportion of Muslim population was 7.60 percent to the total population, which is lower than the National Average.

As per data collected during 2001 Census, there are eight States/Union Territories where the proportion of Muslim population is higher than the National Average. These States/Union Territories are Lakshadweep (95.47%), Jammu and Kashmir (65.23%), Assam (30.92%), West Bengal (25.25%), Kerala (24.70%), Uttar Pradesh (18.50%), Bihar (16.53%) and Jharkhand (13.85%).

In the case of Andaman and Nicobar Islands, Muslim population covers 8.22 percent of the total population. Census 2011 has recorded eight States/Union Territories where the percentage of Muslim population is higher than the National Average. These States/Union Territories are Lakshadweep (96.58%), Jammu and Kashmir (68.31%), Assam (34.22%), West Bengal (27.01%), Kerala (26.56%), Uttar Pradesh (19.26%), Bihar (16.87%) and Jharkhand (14.53%).

During 2011 Census Andaman and Nicobar Islands record 8.52 percent Muslim Population of the total Island population. It is observed that proportion of Muslim population in the Bay Islands has increased steadily from Census 1991 to Census 2011from 7.60 percent to 8.52 percent at par trend of the National Level.

In all the three Censuses i.e. from Census 1991 to Census 2011, Uttar Pradesh scored top position in regard to the Actual number of

Table 3.2: India, States and Union Territories-wise Distribution of Male General and Muslim Population of Census – 1991, 2001 and 2011

Country/States/Union Territoties	Male Population			No. & Percentage of Male Muslim Population					
				1991		2001		2011	
	1991	2001	2011	No.	%	No.	%	No.	%
India	**439,358,440**	**532,223,090**	**623,270,258**	**52,631,365**	**11.98**	**71,374,134**	**13.41**	**88,273,945**	**14.16**
Jammu & Kashmir	NA	5,360,926	6,640,662	NA	—	3,525,446	65.76	4,428,774	66.69
Himachal Pradesh	2,617,467	3,087,940	3,481,873	48,440	1.85	66,173	2.14	80,763	2.32
Punjab	10,778,034	12,985,045	14,639,465	131,284	1.22	213,023	1.64	287,534	1.96
Chandigarh	358,614	506,938	580,663	10,464	2.92	21,539	4.25	29,889	5.15
Uttaranchal	3,640,895	4,325,924	5,137,773	NA	—	539,740	12.48	740,057	14.40
Haryana	8,827,474	11,363,953	13,494,734	407,905	4.62	654,040	5.76	940,027	6.97
Delhi	5,155,512	7,607,234	8,987,326	494,696	9.60	911,006	11.98	1,163,934	12.95
Rajasthan	23,042,780	29,420,011	35,550,997	1,835,622	7.97	2,482,394	8.44	3,193,530	8.98
Uttar Pradesh	70,396,062	87,565,369	104,480,510	12,709,330	18.05	16,028,562	18.30	19,867,314	19.02
Bihar	33,838,238	43,243,795	54,278,157	6,598,961	19.50	7,061,908	16.33	9,044,086	16.66
Sikkim	216,427	288,484	323,070	2,735	1.26	5,346	1.85	6,536	2.02
Arunachal Pradesh	465,004	579,941	713,912	7,788	1.67	12,726	2.19	15,553	2.18
Nagaland	641,282	1,047,141	1,024,649	12,864	2.01	21,690	2.07	28,527	2.78
Manipur	938,359	1,161,952	1,438,586	68,201	7.27	96,787	8.33	120,404	8.37
Mizoram	358,978	459,109	555,339	4,126	1.15	7,946	1.73	9,550	1.72
Tripura	1,417,930	1,642,225	1,874,376	100,799	7.11	130,788	7.96	160,930	8.59
Meghalaya	907,687	1,176,087	1,491,832	32,887	3.62	52,455	4.46	67,827	4.55
Assam	11,657,989	13,777,037	15,939,443	3,289,295	28.21	4,252,691	30.87	5,463,393	34.28
West Bengal	35,510,633	41,465,985	46,809,027	8,360,835	23.54	10,470,406	25.25	12,640,092	27.00
Jharkhand	11,363,853	13,885,037	16,930,315	NA	—	1,924,730	13.86	2,467,219	14.57
Orissa	16,064,146	18,660,570	21,212,136	298,062	1.86	391,234	2.10	465,992	2.20
Chhattisgarh	8,872,620	10,474,218	12,832,895	NA	—	210,829	2.01	263,834	2.06
Madhya Pradesh	25,394,673	31,443,652	37,612,306	1,706,443	6.72	1,991,181	6.33	2,454,832	6.53
Gujarat	21,355,209	26,385,577	31,491,260	1,853,002	8.68	2,370,832	8.99	3,007,221	9.55

contd...

Daman & Diu	51,595	92,512	150,301	4,474	8.67	6,827	7.38	11,347	7.55
Dadra & Nagar Haveli	70,953	121,666	193,760	1,824	2.57	3,855	3.17	7,701	3.97
Maharashtra	40,825,618	50,400,596	58,243,056	4,008,934	9.82	5,437,926	10.79	6,789,127	11.66
Andhra Pradesh	33,724,581	38,527,413	42,442,146	3,025,105	8.97	3,562,239	9.25	4,085,913	9.63
Karnataka	22,951,917	26,898,918	30,966,657	2,681,164	11.68	3,302,582	12.28	4,007,871	12.94
Goa	594,790	687,248	739,140	32,927	5.54	49,391	7.19	63,814	8.63
Lakshadweep	26,618	31,131	33,123	24,524	92.13	28,921	92.90	31,166	94.09
Kerala	14,288,995	15,468,614	16,027,412	3,314,687	23.20	3,776,371	24.41	4,176,255	26.06
Tamil Nadu	28,298,975	31,400,909	31,400,909	1,527,137	5.40	1,718,511	5.47	2,099,182	6.69
Pondicherry	408,081	486,961	612,511	25,266	6.19	28,303	5.81	36,450	5.95
Andaman & Nicobar Islands	154,369	192,972	202,871	11,584	7.50	15,736	8.15	17,301	8.53

Muslim population in the country followed by West Bengal. Bihar ranks the third position, even after the bifurcation of Jharkhand State. Least number of Muslim populations is enumerated in Dadra and Nagar Haveli Union Territory during 1991 and 2001 Census. But in 2011 Census, least number of Muslim populations is recorded in Sikkim.

Table 3.2 depicts the distribution of Male General Population and Male Muslim Population with proportion to total Male population at India and States & Union Territories of 1991, 2001 and 2011 Censuses. This Table shows that during the last three Censuses i.e. 1991, 2001 and 2011, the percentage of Male Muslim Population to Total Male Population of the country has recorded 11.98 percent, 13.41 percent and 14.16 percent respectively also shows an increasing trend. During 1991 Census there were six States/Union Territories where proportionate of Male Muslim Population is higher than the National Level (11.98%). These States/Union Territories were Lakshadweep (92.13%), Assam (28.21%), West Bengal (23.54%), Kerala (23.20%), Bihar (19.50%) and Uttar Pradesh (18.05%). Rest of the States and Union Territories of the country were below the National Average.

In Andaman and Nicobar Islands proportionate of Male Muslim Population was 7.50 percent.

As per data collected during Census 2001, there are eight States/Union Territories where the share of Male Muslim Population to the total Male Population is higher than the National Average (13.41%). These States/Union Territories are Lakshadweep (92.90%), Jammu and Kashmir (65.76%), Assam (30.87%), West Bengal (25.25%), Kerala (24.41%), Uttar Pradesh (18.30%), Bihar (16.33%) and Jharkhand (13.86%).

Andaman and Nicobar Islands share only 8.15 percent to the Male Total Population.

Like two previous Censuses i.e. 1991 and 2001, in 2011 Census there are nine States/Union Territories where the proportion of Male

Table 3.3: India and States & Union Territories Distribution of Female General Population and Female Muslim Population of Censuses-1991, 2001 and 2011

Country/States/Union Territories	Female Population			No. & Percentage of Female Muslim Population					
				1991		2001		2011	
	1991	2001	2011	No.	%	No.	%	No.	%
India	**407,062,599**	**496,514,346**	**587,584,719**	**48,964,692**	**9.86**	**66,814,106**	**13.46**	**83,971,213**	**14.29**
Jammu & Kashmir	NA	4,782,774	5,900,640	NA	---	3,267,794	68.32	4,138,711	70.14
Himachal Pradesh	2,553,410	2,989,960	3,392,729	40,694	1.36	53,339	1.78	69,118	2.04
Punjab	9,503,935	11,373,954	13,103,873	108,117	0.95	169,022	1.49	247,955	1.89
Chandigarh	283,401	393,697	474,787	7,013	1.78	14,009	3.56	21,558	4.54
Uttaranchal	3,409,739	4,163,425	4,948,519	NA	---	472,401	11.35	666,768	13.47
Haryana	7,636,174	9,780,611	11,856,728	355,870	3.64	568,876	5.82	841,315	7.10
Delhi	4,265,132	6,243,273	7,800,615	394,945	6.33	712,514	11.41	994,750	12.75
Rajasthan	20,963,210	27,087,177	32,997,440	1,689,717	6.24	2,305,833	8.51	3,021,847	9.16
Uttar Pradesh	61,665,591	78,632,552	95,331,831	11,400,354	14.50	14,711,596	18.71	18,616,653	19.53
Bihar	30,692,316	39,754,714	49,821,295	6,189,024	15.57	6,660,140	16.75	8,513,723	17.09
Sikkim	190,030	252,367	287,507	1,114	0.44	2,347	0.93	3,331	1.16
Arunachal Pradesh	399,554	518,027	669,815	4,134	0.80	7,949	1.53	11,492	1.72
Nagaland	568,264	942,895	953,853	7,778	0.82	13,315	1.41	20,436	2.14
Manipur	898,790	1,131,944	1,417,208	65,334	5.77	94,152	8.32	119,432	8.43
Mizoram	330,778	429,464	541,867	412	0.10	2,153	0.50	5,282	0.97
Tripura	1,339,275	1,556,978	1,799,541	95,696	6.15	123,654	7.94	155,112	8.62
Meghalaya	867,091	1,142,735	1,475,057	28,575	2.50	46,714	4.09	62,572	4.24
Assam	10,756,333	12,878,491	15,266,133	3,083,909	23.95	3,987,920	30.97	5,215,952	34.17

contd...

West Bengal	32,567,332	38,710,212	44,467,088	7,715,001	19.93	9,770,137	25.24	12,014,733	27.02
Jharkhand	10,480,058	13,060,792	16,057,819	NA	—	1,806,578	13.83	2,326,775	14.49
Orissa	15,595,590	18,144,090	20,762,082	279,713	1.54	370,751	2.04	445,678	2.15
Chhattisgarh	8,742,308	10,359,585	12,712,303	NA	—	198,786	1.92	251,164	1.98
Madhya Pradesh	23,171,569	28,904,371	35,014,503	1,576,357	5.45	1,850,268	6.40	2,319,863	6.63
Gujarat	19,954,373	24,285,440	28,948,432	1,753,918	7.22	2,222,022	9.15	2,839,540	9.81
Daman & Diu	49,991	65,692	92,946	4,574	6.96	5,454	8.30	7,930	8.53
Dadra & Nagar Haveli	67,524	98,824	149,949	1,517	1.54	2,669	2.70	5,221	3.48
Maharashtra	38,111,569	46,478,031	54,131,277	3,619,821	7.79	4,832,559	10.40	6,182,025	11.42
Andhra Pradesh	32,783,427	37,682,594	42,138,631	2,898,849	7.69	3,424,617	9.09	3,996,499	9.48
Karnataka	22,025,284	25,951,644	30,128,640	2,552,859	9.84	3,160,545	12.18	3,885,194	12.90
Goa	575,003	660,420	719,405	28,528	4.32	42,819	6.48	57,750	8.03
Lakshadweep	25,089	29,519	31,350	24,241	82.12	28,982	98.18	31,102	99.21
Kerala	14,809,523	16,372,760	17,378,649	3,473,677	21.22	4,087,471	24.97	4,697,217	27.03
Tamil Nadu	27,559,971	31,004,770	36,009,055	1,525,580	4.92	1,752,136	5.65	2,130,297	5.92
Pondicherry	399,704	487,384	635,442	27,601	5.66	31,055	6.37	39,106	6.15
Andaman & Nicobar Islands	126,292	163,180	177,710	9,770	5.99	13,529	8.29	15,112	8.50

Muslim Population to the Total Male Population is greater than the Country's Average. These States/Union Territories are Lakshadweep (94.09%), Jammu and Kashmir (66.69%), Assam (34.28%), West Bengal (27.00%), Kerala (26.06%), Uttar Pradesh (19.02%), Bihar (16.66%), Jharkhand (14.57%) and Uttaranchal (14.40%).

In Andaman and Nicobar Islands, corresponding proportion stands for 8.53 percent.

Table 3.3 depicts that at the National Level Female Muslim population share to total Female population during 1991, 2001 and 2011 Censuses are 9.86 percent, 13.46 percent and 14.29 percent respectively. Sex-wise figure shows the same trend to that of the total population.

During 1991 Census there were six States/Union Territories where Female Muslim population is higher than National Average (9.86%). These States/Union Territories were Lakshadweep (82.12%), Assam (23.95%), Kerala (21.22%), West Bengal (19.93%), Bihar (15.57%) and Uttar Pradesh (14.50%).

The correspondence figure for Andaman and Nicobar Islands was 5.99 percent.

States and Union Territories-wise 2001 Census recorded that there are eight States/Union Territories where Female Muslim population is in the higher proportion than the National Percentage (13.46%). These States/Union Territories are Lakshadweep (98.18%), Jammu and Kashmir (68.32%), Assam (30.97%), West Bengal (25.24%), Kerala (24.97%), Uttar Pradesh (18.71%), Bihar (16.75%) and Jharkhand (13.83%). Rest of the States and Union Territories of India holds below the National Average.

Andaman and Nicobar Islands share only 8.29 percent to total Island Female population.Census 2011 records that there are eight States/Union Territories in the country where percentage of Female Muslim population to the total Female population crossed the National Average (14.29%). These States/Union Territories are Lakshadweep (99.21%), Jammu and Kashmir (70.14%), Assam (34.17%), Kerala (27.03%), West Bengal (27.02%), Uttar Pradesh

Table 3.4: Censuses-1981, 1991-2001 and 2011, India, States and Union Territories Decadal Growth Rate of General and Muslim Population

Country/States/Union Territories	Decadal Growth Rate of General Population			Decadal Growth Rate of Muslim Population		
	1981-1991	1991-2001	2001-2011	1981-1991	1991-2001	2001-2011
India	**23.87**	**21.54**	**17.70**	**34.54**	**36.02**	**24.65**
Jammu & Kashmir	NA	NA	20.43	NA	NA	26.12
Himachal Pradesh	20.79	17.54	12.94	28.05	34.08	25.41
Punjab	20.81	20.10	13.89	42.42	59.58	40.16
Chandigarh	42.16	40.28	17.19	91.74	103.40	44.73
Uttaranchal	23.13	20.41	18.81	NA	NA	38.99
Haryana	27.41	28.43	19.90	45.89	60.11	45.66
Delhi	51.45	47.02	21.21	84.65	82.49	32.96
Rajasthan	28.44	28.41	21.31	41.46	35.82	29.81
Uttar Pradesh	25.61	25.85	20.23	36.54	27.50	25.19
Bihar	23.38	28.62	25.42	29.50	7.30	27.95
Sikkim	28.47	33.06	12.89	18.76	NA	28.26
Arunachal Pradesh	36.83	27.00	26.03	135.01	NA	30.81
Nagaland	56.08	64.53	-0.58	74.84	69.58	39.87
Manipur	29.29	24.86	24.50	34.44	42.99	25.61
Mizoram	39.70	28.82	23.48	105.80	NA	46.87
Tripura	34.30	16.03	14.84	41.84	29.48	24.22
Meghalaya	32.86	30.65	27.95	528.24	-61.90	31.49
Assam	24.24	18.92	17.07	NA	29.30	29.59
West Bengal	24.73	17.77	13.84	36.89	25.91	21.81

contd...

Jharkhand	24.03	23.36	22.42	NA	NA	28.48
Odisha	20.06	16.25	14.05	36.83	31.88	19.64
Chhattisgarh	25.73	18.27	22.61	NA	NA	25.73
Madhya Pradesh	27.24	24.26	20.35	31.21	17.02	24.29
Gujarat	21.19	22.66	19.28	24.70	27.33	27.30
Daman & Diu	28.62	55.73	53.76	NA	35.73	56.97
Dadra & Nagar Haveli	33.57	59.22	55.88	70.15	95.27	98.07
Maharashtra	25.73	22.73	15.99	31.78	34.63	26.30
Andhra Pradesh	24.20	14.59	10.98	30.85	17.94	15.68
Karnataka	21.12	17.51	15.60	27.57	23.48	22.12
Goa	16.08	15.21	8.23	NA	50.04	31.83
Lakshadweep	28.47	17.30	6.30	28.53	18.74	7.54
Kerala	14.32	9.43	4.91	24.74	15.84	12.84
Tamil Nadu	15.39	11.72	15.61	21.50	9.16	21.86
Pondicherry	33.64	20.62	28.08	47.17	12.28	27.29
Andaman & Nicobar Islands	48.70	26.90	6.86	29.10	37.05	10.76

(19.53%), Bihar (17.02%) and Jharkhand (14.49%).

For Andaman and Nicobar Islands this figure stands for 8.50% which is much below the National Average.

From Table 3.1, Table 3.2 and Table 3.3 it is observed that sex-wise figure shows the same trend in respect of both proportion and actual number as in case of total population.

Table 3.4 shows the distribution of Decadal Growth Rate of General Population and Muslim Population of the Country, States and Union Territories of the three Census decades i.e. 1981-1991, 1991-2001 and 2001-2011.

Decadal Growth Rate for the overall population at the National Level is23.87, 21.54 and 17.70 respectively for the period during 1981-1991, 1991-2001 and 2001-2011.

India and States & Union Territories Decadal Growth rate of General Population and Muslim Population of during – 1981-1991, 1991-2001 and 2001-2011.

During the same period i.e. 1981-1991, 1991-2001 and 2001-2011, Decadal Growth Rate for the Muslim population at the National Level is much higher in all the three decades in comparison to the Decadal Growth Rate of General population which are 34.54, 36.02 and 24.65 respectively.

During 1981-1991, Decadal Growth Rate for Muslim population was 34.54 at the National level. There are fifteen States and Union Territories where the Decadal Growth Rate of Muslim population has crossed the Country's Decadal Growth Rate. These States and Union Territories are Meghalaya (528.24), Arunachal Pradesh (135.01), Mizoram (105.80), Chandigarh (91.74), Delhi (84.65), Nagaland (74.84), Dadra and Nagar Haveli (70.15), Pondicherry (47.17), Haryana (45.89), Punjab (42.42), Tripura (41.84), Rajasthan (41.46), Jharkhand (36.89), Oddisa (36.86) and Uttar Pradesh (36.54).

For Andaman and Nicobar Islands it is 29.10 which is much below the National Average.

State and Union Territories-wise Decadal Growth Rate for the Muslim population for the period 1991-2001 shows that there are ten States and Union Territories where Decadal Growth Rate is higher than the Decadal Growth Rate at the National Level. These States and Union Territories are Chandigarh (103.40), Dadra and Nagar Haveli (95.27), Delhi (82.49), Nagaland (69.58), Meghalaya (61.90), Haryana (60.11), Punjab (59.58), Goa (50.04), Manipur (42.99) and Andaman and Nicobar Islands (37.05).

Decadal Growth Rate for the period 2001-2011 of Muslim population has recorded that the majority of States and Union Territories have Decadal Growth Rate higher than the National Decadal Growth Rate. These States and Union Territories are Dadra and Nagar Haveli (98.07), Daman and Diu (56.97), Mizoram (46.87), Haryana (45.66), Chandigarh (44.73), Punjab (40.16), Nagaland (39.87), Uttaranchal (38.99), Delhi (32.96), Goa (31.83), Meghalaya (31.49) Arunachal Pradesh (30.81), Rajasthan (29.81), Assam (29.58), Jharkhand (28.48), Sikkim (28.26), Bihar (27.95), Gujarat (27.30), Pondicherry (27.29), Jammu and Kashmir (26.12), Manipur (25.61), Himachal Pradesh (25.41), Uttar Pradesh (25.19), Chhattisgarh (25.73) and Maharashtra (26.30).

Table 3.5 shows the distribution of district-wise General population and Muslim population of three Censuses i.e. 1991, 2001 and 2011. District-wise Muslim population of Andaman and Nicobar Islands reflects that the majority of Muslim population is enumerated in the Andaman District in all the three Censuses which are 94.73 percent, 92.72 percent and 95.88 percent respectively. Muslim population in Nicobar District is recorded during Census 1991, Census 2001 and Census 2011 as 5.27 percent, 7.28 percent and 4.12 percent respectively.

Table 3.6 reveals that Decadal Growth Rate for General population during the Census decades of 1981-1991, 1991-2001 and 2001-2011 of Andaman and Nicobar Islands. Andaman district always registered higher Decadal Growth Rate than the Nicobar district. Both the districts recorded a decreasing Decadal Growth Rate.

Table 3.5: District-wise Distribution of General and Muslim Population of Censuses 1991, 2001, 2011 of Andaman and Nicobar Islands

U.T. / District	Population			No. & Percentage of Muslim Population		
	1991	2001	2011	1991	2001	2011
Andaman & Nicobar Islands	280,661	356,152	380,581	21,354 (7.61)	29,265 (8.22)	32,413 (8.52)
Andaman	241,453	314,084	343,739	20,228 (94.73)	27,134 (92.72)	31,077 (95.88)
Nicobar	39,208	42,068	36,842	1,126 (5.27)	2,131 (7.28)	1,336 (4.12)

For Census, 2011	Population	No. & Percentage of Muslim Population
North and Middle Andaman District	105,597	2,165 (2.05%)
South Andaman District	238,142	28,912 (12.14%)

Table 3.6: District-wise Decadal Growth rate of General and Muslim Population during 1981-1991, 1991-2001 and 2001-2011 of Andaman and Nicobar Islands

U.T. / District	Decadal Growth Rate of General Population			Decadal Growth Rate of Muslim Population		
	1981-1991	1991-2001	2001-2011	1981-1991	1991-2001	2001-2011
Andaman & Nicobar Islands	48.70	26.90	6.86	31.91	37.05	10.76
Andaman	52.54	30.08	9.44	32.29	34.14	14.53
Nicobar	28.74	7.29	-12.42	25.33	89.25	-37.31

District-wise Decadal Growth Rate of Muslim population of Andaman and Nicobar Islands shows that there is an increasing trend in both the districts during 1981-1991 and 1991-2001.In the Andaman district it is recorded as 32.29 and 34.14 respectively while for Nicobar district the corresponding figures are 25.33 and 89.25.But during 2001-2011, the Decadal Growth Rate has not increased; particularly in the Nicobar district. Negative Decadal Growth Rate is observed both for the General Population and Muslim Population – probably the effect of Tsunami is the reason.

As the Census does not publish Community-wise Religion data, so it is not possible to show distribution of Muslim population in different community level. As per my observation, when I was posted in the Anthropological Survey of India, A&N Islands Regional Centre, majority of Muslim population is the Bay Islands belongs to Moplah Community. "Local Born" share a small proportion of Muslim population. Among the Nicobarese, a negligible percentage follow/embrace Muslim Religion.

The word 'Moplah' is derived from the Arabic word *ma fella* which means non-cultivators. Moplah or Mopla are also known as 'Mappila'. Outsiders also refer them as 'Kaka'. In the ninth century AD Muslim traders from Arabia and other West Asian countries came to India to trade in spices. They have to stay in India for long, get married and their children are known as the Moplah as claimed by the people of this community.

After World War-I, many Indian Muslims joined the Non Co-operation Movement launched by Indian National Congress which resulted in the outbreak of the Moplah Rebellion in August, 1921. The British Government decided to deport the rebels to Andamans. They were allowed to take their women with them. They settled in villages of South Andamans where still people of this community are found. According to 1931 Census when the last community-wise figures were published, it is seen that the Moplah community are found in the villages like Bambooflat, Stewartgunj, Govindapuram, Wimberlygunj, Mannarghat, Wright Myo, Ograbranj, Malapuram, Calicut and Panighat of South Andaman district.

Malayalam is the mother tongue of the Moplah community. They also speak Hindi, Tamil, Telugu, Urdu, Arabic and some of them English. They use the Latin and Devanagari scripts for correspondence. In the Andaman and Nicobar Islands they enjoy 'Local' status as framed by the Administration of the Andaman and Nicobar Islands. The staple food of the Moplah is rice. They eat millet, pulses, oilseeds and a lot of coconuts, bananas, roots and tubers. They also grow vegetables in their kitchen gardens which they use to consume. They eat beef but not pork. Moplah people use to drink tea and milk but generally they do not drink alcohol. Adult male smoke *beedis* and cigarettes and also chew tobacco (*khaini*). Some elderly women also smoke *beedis*.

The Moplahs are divided into three religious groups i.e. Sunni, Wahabi and Quadiani. Although member of Quadiani sect are very few in number, inter-marriage is allowed between the first two. Each sect follows certain distinct rituals concerning marriage, death and religious celebrations. The senior-most male member is designated as the Head of the Family. Managing the household is entirely the wife's privilege. Women also take part in agricultural activities. They also graze cattle. They contribute economically to the family and enjoy equal status. They are allowed to have a voice in political affairs. However, in religious activities the women have a subordinate status. They do not have the right to go to the mosque. Moplahs are primarily agriculturist and have individual owned lands. Paddy is the main crop grown. Rain water is the main source of irrigation. Some Moplahs grow coconuts, betel nuts, fruits, vegetables etc.

The Moplah have a traditional village council of their own which is composed of selected four elderly person of the community to settle all kind of disputes, to maintain law and order and also to work for the welfare of the community. Women are not allowed to be a member of the council. From 1961 the statutory Gram Panchayat system was introduced to do work for the welfare and development of the villagers. The Moplah have their own folk art tradition largely based on religion. This is practiced by both men and women, to the accompaniment of string instruments.

With the passing of time, today the Moplah children are going to school. Through National Rural Development Programmes and other Government Schemes some of them are getting employed. They have got radios and televisions. Melted roads are built inside their villages. Villages are electrified. Nutrition programmes for children and pregnant and nursing mothers are availed of through the Integrated Child Development Schemes. There are ration shops in the locality and today they also avail banking facilities.

REFERENCES

Banthia, J.K. (2004), *Census of India 2001, India, The First Report on Religion Data*, Office of the Registrar General, India, New Delhi.

Coomar, P.C. (1994), *Moplas* in People of India, Andaman and Nicobar Islands, Vol. 12, pp. 122-129, Calcutta, Affiliated East West Press Pvt. Ltd.

Mayeeb, M. (1972), *Islamic Influence on Indian Society*, Delhi, Meenakshi Prakashan.

Rahman, Z. (2000), Religion and Culture in the Lives of Indian Muslims. *The Eastern Anthropologist*, Vol. 53, No. 3-4.

Sakir, M. (1970), *Khilafat to Partition*, New Delhi, Kalamkar Prakashan.

Verma, V.S. (1984), *Census of India 1981, India, Series-1, Household Population By Religion of Head of Household*, Office of the Registrar General, India, New Delhi.

www.censusindia.gov.in

4

A Study on Socio-Economic Status of Muslims in India

Ajitha Narendran and K. Rajmohan

Introduction

India is a country with diversities inhabiting various ethnic, cultural, linguistic and religious groups. The development of education varies among these groups. The Constitution of India aims to bridge these gaps by empowering the society and providing equality of status among all citizens. These ideas are reflected in different articles of the constitution and to realise these ideas different policies, programmes and schemes have been initiated by the Government of India (GOI). In India the National Minority Commission has identified Muslims as 'Muslims' as minorities along with Christians, Sikhs, Buddhists and Jains on the basis of religion. Out of these religious minorities Muslims are the largest ones. In spite of being the largest minority, they are lagging behind in education in comparison with other religious minorities.

Meaning of Minority

No definition of the term minority has so far received universal approval.

A Minority is therefore, typically in a state of marginalisation, a condition which, in turn, restricts realisation of its creative potential. Minorities have a special place in the development of India. The percentage of population of minorities is not less than 20 percent of the country. Among, all the minorities, Muslim Community are the most backward in terms of education and economic means. One of the most important reasons of the backwardness of Indian Muslims is the lack of education.

The three-fold problems of minority are:

- *Security:* First and foremost, it is necessary, that every minority group is assured of a complete sense of security from fear, limb and property.
- *Economic Opportunities*: There can be no social equality without approximate economic equality. The conscious discrimination in employment in services and admission in schools and colleges should be done away with.
- *Social upliftment*: The thrust of all new policies today must be towards progressive realisation of all social welfare aims and objectives. The traditional inequalities should be removed.

Objectives of the Study

The following are the main objectives of the study:

- To study the present status of the Indian Muslims.
- To study the socio-economic conditions of the Indian Muslims.
- To identify whether the Muslims have adequate access to education, health services, municipal infrastructure and bank credit.
- To determine the relative share in public and private sector employment.
- To study the findings of the Sachar Committee.
- To identify the recommendations and suggestions made by the Sachar Committee.

- To find out the problems of Indian Muslims.
- To find out the reasons behind the backwardness of Indian Muslims.

Methodology

This study is purely based on secondary data particularly the Report of the Sachar Committee and other related articles.

Disagreement of Muslims and Non-Muslims

In the Indian context, economic conditions along with community and caste affiliations present themselves as appropriate variables that should go into defining these groups. Consequently taking a lead from the Sachar Committee, Socio-Religious Communities (SRCs) within both Muslims and non-Muslims population are sought to be defined in a fairly disaggregated manner. Using the National Sample Survey Organisation (NSSO), separate categories have been defined. This disaggregates Hindus into:

- Hindu, Upper Caste ⟶ Hindu (UC)
- Hindu, Other Backward Classes ⟶ Hindu (OBCs)
- Hindu, Scheduled Castes ⟶ Hindu (SC)
- Hindu, Scheduled Tribes ⟶ Hindu (ST)

Muslims are divided into General and OBCs (including those Muslims that report their caste as SC) groups.

- Muslim, General ⟶ Muslim (Gen)
- Muslims, OBC ⟶ Muslim (OBC)

Other Minorities are retained as separate category.

The Present Status of Muslims

The Minority religious groups as identified by the National Minority Commission constitute 18 percent of the total population of the country where Muslims are the largest religious minority and constitute 13.4 percent of the population as per census 2001. It has now increased to 14.25 in 2011, which shows that the population of Muslims rose by 0.8 percent from 2001 to 2011. Nevertheless, despite being the largest religious minority, Muslim literacy rate is the lowest among all the religious minorities. Data's shows that Muslim in India is more likely to have three or more children are living at home. These growing minorities of Muslim Indians are more economically disadvantaged and dissatisfied than Indians of other religious groups. Muslims are more likely than the Indian population overall to be below poverty line.

India now has 966.3 million Hindus, who make up 79.8 percent of its population, and 172.2 million Muslims, who make up 14.23 percent. Among the other minorities, Christians make up 2.3 percent of the population and Sikhs 1.72 percent. The Registrar-General and Census Commissioner released this data on Population by Religious Communities of Census 2011. The distribution of data is of the total population by six major religious communities — Hindu, Muslim, Christian, Sikh, Buddhist and Jain — besides "Other religions and persuasions" and "Religion not stated".

The increase in State-wise Muslim population is tabulated above, which shows that there is an overall increase of 0.8 percent from 2001 to 2011.

Interestingly, Pondicherry was the only state to show a fall in Muslim population as a percentage of its total population (a fall of 0.4 percentage points). Nationally, percentage of Muslims in total population went up from 13.4 percent in 2001 to 14.3 percent in 2011. Assam recorded highest increased in share of Muslims, from 30.9 percent of the state population to 34.2 percent.

The sex ratio among Muslims now stands at 951 females for every 1, 000 males, substantially better than 936 in 2001, while among Hindus, it is 939 females for every 1,000 males during 2011, a slight improvement over the 2001 value of 931. J&K remains the State with the largest Muslim population as a proportion (68.31 percent) and saw the largest increase in the Muslim proportion between 2001 and 2011, followed by Assam 34.22 percent and West

Table 4.1: India, States and Union Territories-wise Decadal Growth rate of General and Muslim Population during 1981-1991, 1991-2001 and 2001-2011.

Country/States/Union Territories	Decadal Growth Rate of General Population			Decadal Growth Rate of Muslim Population		
	1981-1991	1991-2001	2001-2011	1981-1991	1991-2001	2001-2011
India	**23.87**	**21.54**	**17.70**	**34.54**	**36.02**	**24.65**
Jammu & Kashmir	NA	NA	20.43	NA	NA	26.12
Himachal Pradesh	20.79	17.54	12.94	28.05	34.08	25.41
Punjab	20.81	20.10	13.89	42.42	59.58	40.16
Chandigarh	42.16	40.28	17.19	91.74	103.40	44.73
Uttaranchal	23.13	20.41	18.81	NA	NA	38.99
Haryana	27.41	28.43	19.90	45.89	60.11	45.66
Delhi	51.45	47.02	21.21	84.65	82.49	32.96
Rajasthan	28.44	28.41	21.31	41.46	35.82	29.81
Uttar Pradesh	25.61	25.85	20.23	36.54	27.50	25.19
Bihar	23.38	28.62	25.42	29.50	7.30	27.95
Sikkim	28.47	33.06	12.89	18.76	NA	28.26
Arunachal Pradesh	36.83	27.00	26.03	135.01	NA	30.81
Nagaland	56.08	64.53	-0.58	74.84	69.58	39.87
Manipur	29.29	24.86	24.50	34.44	42.99	25.61
Mizoram	39.70	28.82	23.48	105.80	NA	46.87
Tripura	34.30	16.03	14.84	41.84	29.48	24.22
Meghalaya	32.86	30.65	27.95	528.24	-61.90	31.49
Assam	24.24	18.92	17.07	NA	29.30	29.59
West Bengal	24.73	17.77	13.84	36.89	25.91	21.81
Jharkhand	24.03	23.36	22.42	NA	NA	28.48
Odisha	20.06	16.25	14.05	36.83	31.88	19.64
Chhattisgarh	25.73	18.27	22.61	NA	NA	25.73
Madhya Pradesh	27.24	24.26	20.35	31.21	17.02	24.29

contd...

Gujarat	21.19	22.66	19.28	24.70	27.33	27.30
Daman & Diu	28.62	55.73	53.76	NA	35.73	56.97
Dadra & Nagar Haveli	33.57	59.22	55.88	70.15	95.27	98.07
Maharashtra	25.73	22.73	15.99	31.78	34.63	26.30
Andhra Pradesh	24.20	14.59	10.98	30.85	17.94	15.68
Karnataka	21.12	17.51	15.60	27.57	23.48	22.12
Goa	16.08	15.21	8.23	NA	50.04	31.83
Lakshadweep	28.47	17.30	6.30	28.53	18.74	7.54
Kerala	14.32	9.43	4.91	24.74	15.84	12.84
Tamil Nadu	15.39	11.72	15.61	21.50	9.16	21.86
Pondicherry	33.64	20.62	28.08	47.17	12.28	27.29
Andaman & Nicobar Islands	48.70	26.90	6.86	29.10	37.05	10.76

Bengal 27.01 percent.

Table 4.2: Distribution of Religion-wise Population and Percentage of Total Population at National level during Census, 2011

Religion	Numbers of total Population	
Hindu	966257353	79.80%
Muslim	172245153	14.23%
Christian	27819588	2.30%
Sikh	20833116	1.72%
Buddhist	8442972	0.70%
Jain	4451753	0.37%
Other Religions and Persuasions (ORP)	7937734	0.65%
Religion Not Stated	2867303	0.24%
Total	**1210854977**	**100.00%**

Educational Status of Muslims

Education has always played a very important role in every society. It makes an individual to internalise the values and the norms of the society and simultaneously offers the specific skilled persons to serve different functions in the society. The role of education facilitating social and economic progress is well accepted today. Improvement in education opens up opportunities leading to both individual and group entitlements. Education is essential for lifting the population out of poverty. The country needs an educated workforce to fill the skilled jobs created as India's economy grows.

Indian Muslims are at an educational disadvantage in a country where achieved levels of education are generally very low. Muslims are at a double disadvantage with low level of education combined with low quality of education. According to the Sachar Committee Report, this includes:

- Creating high quality Government schools in all areas of Muslim concentration.
- Opening schools that are exclusively for girls particularly for grades IX to XII.

- In Co-Educational schools, hiring more female teachers.
- Make primary school education available in Urdu, as this is the mother language of many Muslims and education in one's native tongue is constitutionally mandated in India.

Increased educational attainment for women has the additional benefits of reducing the fertility rate, thereby increasing opportunities for economic development, mitigating health risks for women and children, and improving quality of life, particularly for women. The following indicators have been used to analyse the educational status of Muslims in India:

Literacy rates, enrolment rates, Higher education and Dropout rates or Mean year of schooling

Literacy Rates

The literacy rate among the Muslims in 2001 is 68.54 percent which is very low, below the national average of 72.98 percent with the gap greatest in urban areas. The literacy rates among Muslim women are 50 percent. It is also found that the female literacy rate is very low and they are educationally more backward as compared to males. The literacy rate as per Census 2001 of all communities is shown in the Table 4.3.

According to the Ministry of Minority Affairs, Government of India, the literacy rates among Muslims has improved from 1999-2000 to 2007-08. Literacy among Muslims increased from 52.1 percent in 1999-2000 to 63.5 percent in 2007-08 in rural areas and from 69.8 percent to 75.1 percent in urban areas. According to the Ministry, the literacy rate of Muslims as a ratio of the national average has also gone up from 0.93 in 1999-2000 to 0.95 in 2007-08 for rural areas and from 0.87 to 0.89 in 2007-08 for urban areas. This is shown in Table 4.4:

Table 4.3: Literacy Rate of Hindu, Muslims, Schedule Castes and Schedule Tribes and others at the National Level during Census, 2001

	All India	Rural			Urban		
		Total	Male	Female	Total	Male	Female
All	64.8	59	71	46	80	86	73
Hindu	65.1	59	72	46	81	88	74
SC/ST	52.2	49	61	36	68	78	58
Muslims	59.1	53	62	43	70	76	63
Others	70.8	64	77	52	85	90	78

Table 4.4. Literacy Rate among Muslims by Place of Residence during the Period 1999-2000 and 2007-2008 at the National Level

Muslims	1999-2000	2007-08
Rural Areas	52.1%	63.5%
Urban Areas	69.8%	75.1%
Literacy Rate as ratio of National Average (Rural Areas)	0.93	0.95
Literacy Rate as ratio of National Average (Urban Areas)	0.87	0.89

Enrolment Rates

Although the Census of 2001 does not provide the data related to enrolment of children. Data provided by National Sample Survey Organisation (NSSO) and National Council of Applied Economic Research, Human Development Survey (2004-05) has been used to analyse the rate of enrolment of all SRCs. It was concluded that on the basis of data the enrolment ratio has increased in all SRCs. But this advancement is low 65 percent among Muslims as compared to SC and ST (95% increase).

The report also noted that despite a common belief that a large number of Muslim children attend *Madarasa* for primary education, only three percent of Muslim children among the school going age go to *Madarasa*. Instead many Muslim children are enrolled in *Maktabs*, which provide supplementary religious education in addition to enrolment in public schools.

Similarly, the percentage of enrolment of Muslim children to total enrolment at upper primary level which was 8.54 percent in 2007-2008, has increased up to 10.9 percent in rural areas and 13.76 percent for urban areas as per October 2013.

Higher Education

As far as the enrolment ratio of Muslim women is concerned no statistical data has been analysed. The aggregate attainment level of education among Muslim in rural areas is often lower than those of SCs and STs. The overall progress of Muslim women of rural areas in graduate attainment is very low which indicates that the females in rural areas are more deprived of higher education. Specially Muslim women are more, backward when compared to Muslim men.

Dropout Rates and Mean Year of Schooling

The dropout rates is high among Muslims because there is a common belief that Muslim parents feel that education is not important for girls and it may instil a wrong set of values. Even if girls are enrolled they are withdrawn at an early age to marry them off. This leads to higher dropout rates among Muslim girls. The other reasons cited for high dropout rates among Muslim girls is related with non-availability of schools within easy reach of girls at lower level of education, absence of girls hostel, absence of female teachers and non-availability of scholarships as they move up the educational ladder.

A comparison across socio-religious communities both by gender and by place of residence also reveals constantly lower level of mean year schooling for the Muslim community. It was also explored that the differential in mean year schooling between Muslim boys and girls is higher irrespective of rural and urban population.

Economy and Employment

Availability of employment provides an individual and his

(her) family with purchasing power enabling him (her) to acquire subsistence as well as consumption goods to satisfy the basic needs, comforts and leisures. Worker population ratio for Muslim communities is significantly lower than for all other SRCs in rural areas but only marginally lower in urban areas. The lower ratios are due to much lower participation in economic activity by Muslim women. To summarise the economic and employment status of Indian Muslim Workers, data of NSSO (61St Round) has been used.

The economic status has been discussed on the basis of the following indicators:

- Work Participation and Employment rate.
- Types of enterprises Muslims are involved in and location of work.
- Industrial occupational desirability of the workforce.
- The level of earning security of employment conditions.

Work Participation and Employment Rate

The Work Participation Rate (WPR) among Muslims is lower as compared to other SRCs both in rural and urban areas. Aggregate WPR in economic activity by women is low in Muslim community. Therefore, the lower ratios are mainly due to lower participation by Muslim women in economic activity.

Types of Enterprises Muslims are Involved in and Location of Work

According to the Sachar Committee report, "the important striking feature is the comparatively relatively high share of Muslim workers engaged in self-employment activity". As far as concentration in self-employment related activities is concerned, Muslims have fairly high concentration in self-employment activities. Muslim share constitutes 61 percent as compared to 55 percent Hindus engaged in self-employment.

Muslims have very low share in regular jobs in large private enterprises and these differentials are very high between Muslim men and women. The share of Muslim men and women in regular works in public and private sector job is quite low as compared to other SRCs. As compared to SRCs, much larger proportions of Muslims' (both males and females) work in self-owned propriety enterprises in rural area; similar trend is also found in urban area. Muslim men and women are engaged in inferior jobs such as clerical or group C or D posts as compared to Hindu men and women.

Participation of Muslim workers in the informal sector is much higher than the average population, and the percent of Muslim women working within their homes (70%) is much higher than all workers (51%).

Muslim participation rates in security related activities such as the police was 4 percent as compared to SCs and STs at 12 percent and OBCs at 23 percent each.

Table 4.5: Percentage Muslims of Total Population Engaged in Government-Related Employment

Sl. No.	Government-related Employment	Muslims (percent)
1.	Indian Administrative Service	3.0
2.	Indian Foreign Service	1.8
3.	IPS/Security Agencies ,Indian Police Service	4.0
4.	Indian Railways	4.5
5.	Education Department (State Level)	6.5
6.	Home Department (State Level)	7.3
7.	Police Constables	6.0
8.	Health Department	4.5
9.	Transport Department	6.5
10.	Judiciary Employment	7.8

The overall participation of Muslims in Central Government departments and agencies is very low. There is not even a single state in India where the representation of Muslims in the government department matches their population share.

Accessibility of Bank Credit

Discrimination by both public sector and private sector banks in providing bank credit is widespread and the issues were raised in most of the states. It was alleged in some states, that many banks had designated Muslim concentration areas as "Negative Geographical Zones or Red Zones" where bank credit and other facilities were not easily provided. Moreover, Muslims also find it extremely difficult to get a guarantee from the Government officials (which is the stipulated requirement laid down by the banks) as they do not have easy access to the government officials either because there are not enough Muslims in the government sector or because the non-Muslims Government officials are not willing to give them guarantees. This affects the poor Muslims the most.

The Sachar Committee reports that the access of Muslims to bank credit is low and inadequate. The average credit is low compared with others SRCs. The 2001 Census shows that percentage of households availing banking facilities is much lower in villages with high Muslim population.

The average amount lent per account to Muslims is about half that of the other Minorities, and one-third of 'Others'. The Sachar Committee report states, that the financial exclusion of Muslims has far reaching implication for their social-economic and educational upliftment. Steps should be taken to specifically direct credit to Muslims, create awareness of various credit schemes and bring transparency in reporting of information. The following table shows the total percentage of amount outstanding among all communities:

Table 4.6: Distribution of Outstand Amount in Percentage of Muslim Religious Groups and other Minorities Group in both Private Sector and Public Sector Banks.

Banks	Muslims	Other Minorities	Others
Private sector banks	6.6%	7.9%	85.5%
Public Sector banks	4.6%	6.3%	89.1%

Access to Social and Physical Infrastructure

There is an inverse relationship between the proportion of Muslims population and availability of educational infrastructures in small villages. Studies found that as compared to Muslim majority areas, the areas inhabited by fewer Muslims had better roads, local bus stops, *pucca* houses, sewage drainage and water supply facilities.

The Sachar Committee highlighted

- One-third of small villages with high concentration of Muslims do not have any educational institutions.
- About 40 percent of large villages with substantial Muslim concentration do not have any medical facilities.

Poverty

Muslims face fairly high levels of poverty. Their conditions on the whole are slightly better than those of SCs/STs, though slightly worse in urban areas. According to NSSO data, overall 22.7 percent of India's population was poor in 2004-05 (251 million people), with SCs/STs together as the worst off at (35%), followed by Muslims at 31 percent. It is found by the Sachar Committee that substantially a large proportion of the Muslim households in urban areas are in the less than Rs. 500 expenditure bracket. Poverty among Muslims has declined in rural areas by 12 percent whereas the economic conditions of Muslims in urban areas have not improved as much as those of other SRCs.

Findings of the Sachar Committee

The following are the findings of the Sachar Committee:

- Low educational achievement among Muslims is due to the fact that they do not see education as necessarily translating into formal employment.

- Schools beyond the primary level are few in Muslim localities. Exclusive girls' schools are fewer, and are usually at a distance from the Muslim localities.
- Muslims find it difficult to get loans from the banks as many banks have designated most of Muslim concentration areas as "negative or red zones", where they do not give loans. This affects the Muslims the most.
- Muslim presence in private sector was found to be even more dismal. Private sector needs to be sensitised to include Muslims in their recruitment through positive discrimination and affirmative action.
- Absence of proper amenities and infrastructure facilities in Muslim concentration areas is another cause of concern across all the states. Poor roads and lack of proper transport, sanitation, water, electricity and public health facilities pervade Muslim concentration localities.
- Out of 593 districts of India in 2001, only nine districts have Muslim population of 75 percent or above. These included Lakshadweep and eight districts from J&K.
- The literacy rate among Muslims (59.1%) in 2001 was far below the national average (65.1%) and other SRCs (70.8%).
- As many as 25% of Muslim children in the 6-14 year age group have either never attended school or dropped out. Muslims have the highest dropout rate in the country.
- Jawahar Navodaya Vidyalayas Scheme in rural areas was expected to reduce the supply side constraints on good quality education. Muslim Participation in these schools too is unsatisfactory.
- Only one out of 25 under-graduate students and one out of 50 post-graduate students is a Muslim in premier colleges.
- Unemployment among Muslim graduates is the highest as compared to other communities in India both among the poor and the non-poor.

Recommendations

The Sachar Committee made a number of recommendations to address the status of the Muslim community in India.

- Setup an equal opportunity commission to look into the grievances of deprived groups like minority.
- Create a nomination procedure to increase participation of minorities in public bodies.
- Increase employment share of Muslims.
- Workout mechanisms to link *Madrasas's* to Higher Secondary School.
- Recognise degrees from *Madrasas's* for eligibility in defence, civil and banking examinations.

Conclusion

Bringing and retaining children in schools, especially girls, demands additional investment in terms of more physical facilities, more female teachers, separate schools for girls, transport and scholarships, etc. When schools are present in Muslim concentrated areas, they need to be well resourced and functional, in terms of regularity and timing for creating meaningful learning experiences for the Muslim in general and Muslim girls in particular. Finally, it is equally necessary for the government to create conducive and safe environment for removing the feeling of discrimination, along with education as factors for development of religious communities, particularly Muslims in India.

REFERENCES

Census Reports, (2001), *The Registrar General, Census Operation of India*, Ministry of Home Affairs.

Census Reports, (2011), *The Registrar General, Census Operation of India*, Ministry of Home Affairs.

M.Burhanuddin Qasmi (2005), *Education of Muslims in India Problems and Prospects.*

Riaz Ahmad (2010) Social Development Report 2010 – The Land Question and the Marginalised.

Sachar Committee Report, (2006). The committee prepared a 403-page report, titled "Social, Economic and Educational Status of the Muslim Community of India: A Report".

Ziauddin Khan (1983), National Integration in India (*Issues and Dimensions*) Associated, Delhi.

5

Educational Advancement of Muslims: Post Sachar Committee Scenario

S.S. Sreekumar

Introduction

Since the Second World War, nations in Asia have experienced some of the fastest economic growth. The development experience in the world over the last century has shown that economic growth cannot be sustained without taking into consideration the social and political development of vulnerable sections, including greater recognition of minority rights. Better minority socioeconomic and political accommodations have contributed to society's overall well being and the sustainability of economic growth. Integrating minorities as part of their development is a challenge of immense magnitude that Asian societies are facing. The United Nations Sub-Committee on Prevention of Discrimination and Protection of Minorities defines the word minority as "only those non-dominant groups in a population, which possess and wish to preserves stable ethnic, religious or linguistic traditions or characteristics markedly different from those of the rest of the population." (Year Book on Human Rights for 1950, 1952, p. 490). One can find three basic aspects of any minority status; numerical inferiority, non-dominant status, and stable features of distinctive identity.

Nevertheless, the term minority is useful to describe populations that are disadvantaged numerically, socially or politically. The most obvious minorities are tribal, ethnic and religious groups. The United Nations Declaration on the Rights of Persons belonging to National, Ethnic, Religious and Linguistic Minorities says that the promotion and protection of the rights of persons belonging to such minorities contribute to the political and social stability of the countries in which they live and furthers participatory development. Development processes should remove or reduce economic and social obstacles and disparities and help maintain peace and stability.

Conceptual Framework: Education and Development

The role of social variables in fostering development has recently received much attention in the development literature. Amartya Sen and Dean Dreze brought out significance of education in terms of functioning and capability. Functioning refers to what a person does and achieves. Capability on the other hand refers to the range of choices and options which a person has in deciding the kind of life he/she wants to lead. These authors refer to the concept of capability deprivation which may be understood as a severe limitation of freedom and over all state of incapacitation to live and perform dignified labour. The expansion of human capabilities can be enhanced by important social opportunities like education and health care. The basic capabilities for human development are leading a long healthy life, being educated and having adequate resources for a standard of living.

Education is understood to be a crucial factor in at least five distinct ways. First, education has been looked upon as an act of learning leading to personal growth and self development, which has an intrinsic value. Secondly, education enables one to participate in a number of other valuable activities like playing sports, reading, participating in local forums of discussions etc. Thirdly, education makes one more socially aware and politically assertive. An educated person is more aware of his/her social needs and political rights and asserts for them both on an individual level and at the collective level which strengthens democratic practice. Fourth, education makes a lasting impact on social processes and enables one to reject and fight against oppressive socio-cultural practices. Fifth, greater literacy and educational empowerment enables emancipation of the marginalised section of society by accommodating them in the mainstream. (Dreze and Sen, 2006). Thus, education is a tool for the empowerment of the marginalised, as it leads to expansion of choices, freedom and real opportunity. The value of basic education as a tool of social affirmation appears to be well seized by the people. Common finding of village studies and household surveys is that education is widely prescribed by members of socially or economically disadvantaged groups as the most promising means of upward mobility of their children (Syed and Nayak, 1971). An educated person is better equipped to overcome vulnerability and marginalisation in modern society, and it is in that sense that education has considerable empowerment value despite all the shortcomings of the present schooling system. Thus, education of any community with no exception to Muslims will not only be helpful for their development but also for the development of the whole nation. Human capital theory suggests that just as a physical capital (machines) augments a person's economic productivity, so human capital acquired through education improves the productivity of individuals. Studies on the sources of economic growth demonstrate persuasively that education plays a major role as a factor in rise of output per individual. Growth of education is considered as a sign of human growth and development.

Literature Review

The studies on educational status of Muslims and their constraints to educational development are practically very negligible. Various research studies have been carried out to explain the reasons for educational backwardness of the Muslim minorities. Ahmed (1980) has analysed the problems of Muslim educational backwardness in contemporary India. His study illustrates the educational status of the Muslims as well as the socio-cultural constraints which they are facing in the context of educational upliftment among them. Ansari (1989), critically examined the educational backwardness of the Indian Muslims. Educational situation as well as the educational problems of Muslim community of India with particular reference to West Bengal has been studied by Mondal (1989). In contemporary world particularly in developing countries modern education is seen as a means and goal for modernisation. (Pandey, 1988).

Lack of adequate number of schools and infrastructural facilities in the Muslim dominated areas was a major factor. There are many settlements where Government schools are lacking and required facilities do not exist in schools as discussed in the education policies. Studies (Government of India : 2006) pointed out that teaching-learning processes and overall schooling environment (teacher-pupil relationship, pupil-pupil relationship etc., are the reasons of low participation of Muslim children. The outcome data does not always throw light on why some children drop out or why some children learn so little even though they have been attending school, and even being promoted from one grade to the next (Government of India : 2012).

Low participation of girls in schools is another notable problem in the education of Muslims. In schools, physical facilities are not available as per the need of the girls and as per the norms and standards laid by the Government. When schools are not available within a walking distance and closer to the place of dwelling, parents are a bit reluctant-due to the feeling of insecurity-to send their girls to a school which is far off. The studies of Jha (2005). Husain (2010) and Abidi and Abbas (2011) have shown that the reasons for educational backwardness of Muslim girls are lack of Government commitment in providing adequate infrastructural facilities in terms of building with a boundary wall, basic amenities, libraries, hostels, etc. Likewise, high teacher student ratio as well as absence of lady teachers in schools restricted the girls from pursuing schooling. Jha and Jingarans (2005) study reveals that Muslim girls are going to *Madarasa* because Government schools are not functioning well, there is inadequate infrastructure, teachers are irregular and disinterested and the schools remain closed very frequently. Therefore, parents prefer to send girls to religious institutions. Studies by Shariff and Razzack (2006) reveal that "the enrolment rates of Muslim girls have steeply fallen relative to the all-India average, especially during and after the decades of the 1990s". (Shariff and Razzack, 2006).

The studies conducted so far reveal that the major causes for educational backwardness are socio-economic factors, gender issues, shortage of female teachers, teaching learning process in schools, drop out of children, and shortages in the implementation of policies and programmes, etc.

Government of India vide Notification dated 23rd October, 1992 notified five religious communities, viz., Muslims, Christians, Sikhs, Buddhists and Zoroastrians (Parsis) as minority communities under Section 2(c) of the National Commission for Minorities Act, 1992. As per 2001 Census reports, the minorities population was 201.03 million constituting 18.4 percent of the total population of the country. A large proportion of the minorities belong to Muslims (13.4%), followed by Christians (2.3%), Sikhs (1.9%), Buddhists (0.8%) and Zoroastrians (0.0069%).

State-wise population data shows that Muslims constitute majority in Lakshadweep and Jammu and Kashmir. There are six states where Muslim population is above the national average of 13.4 percent. These are: Assam (30.9%), West Bengal (25.2%), Kerala (24.6%), Uttar Pradesh (18.55%), Bihar (16.5%) and Jharkhand (13.8%). In absolute numbers, the largest four states in terms of Muslim population are Uttar Pradesh (3.07 crore), West Bengal (2.02 crore), Bihar (1.37 crore), and Maharashtra (1.07 crore).

Christians constitute a majority in Nagaland (90%), Mizoram (87%) and Meghalaya (70.03%). Sikhs are in majority in the state of Punjab, where their population is 60 percent. There is no Buddhist dominated State or UT in the country. (India, MHRD, 2013). It can also be visualised that Muslim's literacy rate is highest (79.67 percent) in Andaman and Nicobar Island but they constitute only 8.22 percent of the total population.

Table 5.1: Percentage Distribution of Muslim Population, Muslim Enrolment, Muslim Girl's Enrolment in India (2011-2013)

State/UT	% of Muslim Population Census 2011	% of Muslim Enrolment in 2010-11	% of Muslim Enrolment in 2011-12	% of Muslim Enrolment in 2012-13	% Girls Enrolment 2010-11	% Girls Enrolment 2011-12	% Girls Enrolment 2012-13
A and N Islands	8.22	7.86	8.09	8.64	49.72	49.98	50.05
Andhra Pradesh	9.17	9.69	10.07	10.33	49.86	50.23	50.03
Arunachal Pradesh	1.88	0.38	0.37	0.68	47.54	43.63	47.57
Assam	30.92	40.29	40.21	40.00	50.11	50.17	49.97
Bihar	16.53	14.38	15.20	15.06	49.50	49.84	50.88
Chandigarh	3.95	5.18	5.08	3.18	48.15	47.75	48.02
Chhattisgarh	1.97	1.27	1.37	1.45	47.75	48.32	47.99
Dadra and Nagar Haveli	2.96	2.86	3.23	3.38	48.82	46.58	45.14
Daman and Diu	7.76	9.20	9.52	9.90	47.25	47.18	45.43
Delhi	11.72	15.74	13.24	16.06	49.50	49.87	48.82
Goa	6.84	9.81	9.48	9.75	47.13	43.14	48.41
Gujarat	9.06	8.58	8.57	8.70	47.72	48.12	48.35
Haryana	5.78	8.65	9.82	10.87	43.59	44.97	48.46

contd...

State/UT	% of Muslim Population Census 2011	% of Muslim Enrolment in 2010-11	% of Muslim Enrolment in 2011-12	% of Muslim Enrolment in 2012-13	% Girls Enrolment 2010-11	% Girls Enrolment 2011-12	% Girls Enrolment 2012-13
Himachal Pradesh	1.97	1.68	1.82	1.73	46.38	46.68	47.67
Jammu and Kashmir	66.97	67.54	68.47	67.38	48.18	48.11	48.18
Jharkhand	13.85	13.62	14.49	13.83	49.44	49.60	49.65
Karnataka	12.23	15.32	15.95	15.93	49.36	49.01	48.83
Kerala	24.70	31.67	31.29	32.04	49.18	49.27	49.01
Lakshadweep	95.47	89.10	99.38	97.70	48.73	48.83	49.15
Madhya Pradesh	6.37	4.64	4.96	5.41	50.64	49.99	48.30
Maharashtra	10.60	12.83	13.59	13.67	48.79	48.80	48.90
Manipur	8.81	7.65	8.97	9.33	50.81	50.23	50.75
Meghalaya	4.28	3.27	3.51	2.27	50.45	48.99	51.16
Mizoram	1.14	0.21	0.42	0.16	40.95	41.90	45.13
Nagaland	1.76	0.64	0.93	0.94	43.29	43.67	44.28
Odisha	2.07	1.59	1.47	1.92	49.41	48.66	48.47
Puducherry	6.09	7.54	7.63	1.41	48.99	47.28	49.67

contd...

Punjab	1.57	1.44	1.59	1.71	45.75	45.27	46.12
Rajasthan	8.47	7.29	8.43	9.24	46.00	47.00	46.81
Sikkim	1.42	0.87	1.26	1.38	40.74	44.44	44.96
Tamil Nadu	5.56	5.54	5.84	5.94	49.10	49.38	49.06
Tripura	7.95	9.76	11.85	12.94	49.46	49.13	48.74
Uttar Pradesh	18.50	10.43	10.18	14.14	48.18	48.03	48.58
Uttarakhand	11.92	17.07	17.59	16.05	47.02	47.12	47.08
West Bengal	25.25	31.67	32.22	32.33	49.89	50.24	50.04
All States	**13.43**	**13.04**	**13.31**	**14.20**	**49.06**	**49.17**	**49.22**

Source: Govt. of India, Ministry of Human Resource Development, Govt. of India, New Delhi.

Educational Advancement of Muslims: Efforts Taken

After the independence (1947), initiatives for educational development for minorities were started in India, in late 1970s, which geared up after the National Policy on Education (NPE), 1986 and its Programme of Action (POA), 1992. Both the NPE and POA emphasised the need of special efforts, "to bring the educationally backward minorities (which include Muslims) on par with the rest of the society and to make them participate fully in the national development activities" (GOI, 1992, p. 9). Many long term and short term programmes were started in the form of affirmative actions to improve the educational status of minorities like: Prime Ministers 15 Point Programme for the Welfare of the Minorities (1983), Area Intensive Programme for Educationally Backward Minorities, Modernisation of *Madrasa,* Maulana Azad Education Foundation Scheme (1989), Free Supply of Books and Stationery and Merit Scholarship, and Pre-examination Coaching scheme for the weaker sections.

India has achieved significant growth and development. It has improved on crucial human development indices such as levels of literacy, education and health. There are indications, however, that not all religious community and social groups (henceforth Socio-Religious Communities – SRCs) have shared equally the benefits of the growth process. Among these, the Muslims, the largest minority in the country are seriously lagging behind on human development indices.

Objectives of the Study

(a) To examine the educational backwardness of Muslim minority ;

(b) to study the observations of the Sachar Committee to improve the educational level of Muslims; and

(c) to examine the challenges/hurdles in the educational advancement of Muslim community.

Educational Level of Muslims

Present day education system has engulfed half of Muslim population and the other half remains away from it and form part of illiterate class. Lack of education is the reason for failure of upward mobility of large section of Muslim population. This is more so in case of OBC section of Muslim community. Certain emphatic observations can be made about educational condition of Muslims, especially OBC Muslims. These are as under:-

1. There is substantially low level of literacy rate among Muslims.
2. The percentage of illiterates among Muslims is higher than Scheduled Castes and Scheduled Tribes i.e. in the age group of 6-17. This indicates that there is greater emphasis on SCs and STs Students than Muslim in the country in terms of facilities, motivation, scholarship etc.
3. Dropout rate among Muslims are highest at school level than other communities. This is more rampant among OBC Muslims.
4. The gap of education level among Muslims and other groups is higher in urban areas, compared to the rural areas. This is because of early indication of the urban Muslim into traditional parental job and lack of school infrastructure in Muslim areas.
5. The change in educational pattern of Scheduled Castes and Scheduled Tribes has increased substantially due to targeted Government and Private efforts. However, such efforts towards Muslim Communities especially OBC Muslims are absent. Hence there is comparatively higher level of educational backwardness among Muslims and more so among OBC Muslims.

Higher Education

The status with respect to their attainment in the field of higher education needs examination. Three levels of education need to be used for this purpose general graduate and above, technical graduates and technical diploma and certificate courses. It can be seen that in all the three levels of education OBC Muslims have a negligible proportion of persons holding a technical/non-technical degree or technical diploma/certificate compared to the Hindu-OBCs. In the case of technical diploma/certificate courses, some Gen-Muslims have done better while OBC Muslims involvement is very low. Muslim-OBCs have the lowest level of achievements in higher education; in general, Hindu-OBCs do better than Muslim-OBCs. Thus, in terms of higher education also, the Muslim-OBCs lag behind Hindu-OBCs and Muslim-Gen.

Sachar Committee Recommendations/Observations on Education

Ministry of Human Resource Development, Government of India (2013) observed "There is also a common belief that Muslim parents feel that education is not important for girls and that it may install a wrong set of values. Even if girls are enrolled they are withdrawn at an early age to marry them off. This leads to a higher drop-out rate among Muslims girls. Our interactions indicate that the problems may lie more in non-availability of schools within easy reach for girls at lower levels of education, absence of female teachers and availability of scholarships as they move up the education ladder. In some cases absence of vital facilities in schools such as toilets keeps the girls away from schools".

According to the Sachar Committee Report (2006) "*Madarsas* (though not a substitute for regular schools) is necessary for Muslims as, apart from providing basic education, they serve as an important instrument of identity maintenance for the Community. Many a time *Madarsas* are the only educational option available to Muslim children, especially in areas where no schools have reached the Muslim masses. Very often children go to the *Madarsas* not out of choice but due to non-availability and inaccessibility of other schools" (p. 17). Some relevant observations of the Committee with regard to education of Muslim community are as follows:

1. There is a need for sharper focus on school education.The literacy rate among Muslims (59.1%) in 2001 was far below the National average (65.1%) and other Socio-Religious Categories (SRC)-70.8 percent.
2. State level estimates suggest that the literacy gap between Muslims and the general average is greater in urban areas and for women.
3. Owing to their socio-economic backwardness, Muslims have not been able to respond to the challenge of improving their educational status, whereas other communities like SCs and STs have been able to reap the benefit in the field of education with active support of the Government.
4. As many as 25 percent of Muslim children in the 6-14 years age group have either never attended school or have dropped out. Muslims have the highest dropout rate in the country.
5. Only 'one out of the 25 Under-Graduate student's and' one out of the 50 Post-graduate student' is a Muslim in premier colleges. The share of Muslims in all courses is low, particularly at the PG level and marginal in the science stream.
6. Un-employment rate among Muslim graduates is the highest as compared to the other communities in India both among the poor and the non-poor.
7. Muslims are at a much larger disadvantage at the higher secondary level education in both rural and urban areas and for both males and females.
8. Only 3 percent of Muslim children among the school going age go to *Madarsas.*
9. Muslim parents are not averse to modern or mainstream education and sending their children to the affordable Government schools. Therefore, the notion that Muslims prefer only *Madarasa* education, is wrong.
10. Recognise degrees from *Madarsas* for eligibility in Defence, Civil and Banking examinations.

11. Efforts should be made to make information widely available through media, especially in the language understood by Muslims, e.g., Urdu and through counseling centres to ensure that the people are aware of the schemes meant for them and can access them.

Challenges/Obstacles in Muslim Education

1. The major challenge in ensuring the right to education for Muslim community in India is the unconventional attitudes and values with little efforts to change the traditional educational system and to acquire knowledge relevant to needs of changing world. The childhood care and concern has instrumental role in moulding the education of the children. As pointed out by UNESCO early childhood care and education improves the quality of school experience for children in primary and basic education (UNESCO, 2011).
2. According to official report 'High dropout rates among Muslim students are worrisome'. As with many Indians, the main reason for educational backwardness of Muslims is abject poverty due to which children are forced to drop out after the first few classes. This is particularly true for Muslim girls. (Govt. of India, 2013).
3. Among key reasons for non-attendance by marginalised groups are: low quality of education, perceived irrelevance of curricula, or poor quality of teaching (*Ibid.*: 2013). As Sachar Committee reports 'Government schools that do exist in Muslim neighbourhoods are merely centers of low quality education for the poor and marginalised. The poor quality of teaching, learning, absentee teachers, in turn, necessitate high cost inputs like private tuitions, particularly in the case of first generation learners from the Muslim community. (Sachar, 2006).
4. NSSO pointed out that there are large numbers of Muslim dominated *Mohallas* in urban areas which do not have a school, particularly a girls' school, as a result of which the drop-out of girls is much higher. Though the access to upper

primary school seems to be better from aggregated data, there appear to be several pockets in which schools are not available within three kms. (UNESCO, 2011).

5. A study of data derived from DISE shows that a predominant proportion of Muslim children attend government schools at primary and upper primary stages. About 68 percent of Muslim children at primary stage and 55.3 percent at upper primary stage attended state/central government and local body schools in 2011-12. Private, aided schools account for very small proportion of Muslim enrolment at primary and upper primary stages. (Govt. of India, 2006).
6. The meager interest of the Government towards Urdu language is another problem of the Muslim education in the country. Sachar Committee reports that overnight the knowledge of Urdu has become more a liability than an asset. Lack of Urdu medium schools, the poor quality of teaching in them, vacancies for teachers unfilled for several years and the recruitment of Hindi teachers in place of Urdu teachers are some of the problems afflicting the teaching of Urdu.
7. The Hindu and the Christian communities had set up a network of good educational institutions which provides general and professional education. The Muslim community has failed to set up such institutions in large numbers to provide its youth with modern education.
8. Affirmative action may not be possible for the entire Muslim community in the existing situation.

Suggestions

1. Efforts should be made to make information widely available through media, especially in the language understood by Muslims, e.g., Urdu and through counseling centres to ensure that the people are aware of the schemes meant for them and can access.
2. Provide recognition and support to minority educational institutions which should ensure an equitable number of seats for girls.

3. Government should open all-girl schools in the vicinity of minority concentration area. This will help all communities- both majority and minority. Even in non-minority concentration areas, exclusive girl's schools are a necessity.
4. Open more technical institutes for Girls in Minority concentrated areas and ensure equitable admission to girls who should not only be relegated to learning traditional skills like stitching, cooking etc, but also trained in modern technology concepts.
5. Skill development initiatives of ITIs and Polytechnics should focus on sectors which have high growth potential and in which the Muslim population is concentrated.
6. Ensure in all decision making educational bodies of State and Central Universities, qualified Muslim women are given equal opportunity to represent at least one post in each State and Central University bodies.
7. NGOs working for minorities, especially for Muslim minority require to be encouraged both financially, administratively and through other incentives.
8. As part of the modernisation of *Madarasas*, efforts can be made to introduce and encourage job oriented education in *Madarsas*. The model followed in West Bengal(In some states like West Bengal, general syllabus is also taught in *Madarsas* and certificates and degrees awarded by *Madarsas* are recognised and can be adopted in other parts. This enables easy migration from *Madarsas* to general education institutions which can contribute positively to provide a better access to quality education for rural and low socio-economic population.
9. Urdu must be available as an optional subject in all Government and Government-aided schools in areas with substantial Urdu-speaking population. Good quality textbooks in Urdu must be provided.

Concluding Remarks

Participation of Muslims was relatively low in the education space but has improved in recent years. The situation in the urban areas is, however, poor. The participation of Muslims in higher education is particularly poor.The Muslims as minority deserves a special attention and equal opportunity to access their share of resources from the mainstream policies and programmes. The civil society organisations and the local self governing bodies have to take initiative in organising sensitisation /awareness programmes among the Muslim community in the rural area. Through these programmes, the community, especially the women folk can be enriched leading to the empowerment of the community in all spheres.Thus, more emphasis has to be given to :

1. Infrastructural facilities, i.e better access to the basic services and amenities in the Muslim dominated areas.
2. Education of Muslim girls-at the school stage and steps to prevent dropouts.
3. Vocational and technical education equipping them to self employment opportunities.
4. Appropriate steps at the grass root level to organise schemes like Self Help Groups, the participation in which ensures greater involvement in developmental activities and ensures social and political mobilisation. This will also help to develop social capital.

REFERENCES

Abidi, A., and S. Abbas (2011), Educational marginalisation of Muslim in a metropolitan: A sociological study of Jamia Nagar Government Schools, New Delhi. *Islam and Muslim Societies: A Social Science Journal*, 4(1).

Ahmed, I. (1980), The problem of Muslim Educational Backwardness in Contemporary India: An Inferential Analysis, Occasional Paper.

Ansari, A. I., (1989), "Muslim Educational Backwardness", in Iqbal A. Ansari (ed.) The Muslim Situation in India, New Delhi, Sterling Publishers Pvt. Ltd.

Govt. of India, (2013), Report of the Standing Committee of National Monitoring Committee for Minorities Education (NMCME), New Delhi (Ministry for Human Resource Development).

Government of India. (2006), Social, Economic and Educational backwardness of Muslims in India: A Report of the Prime Minister's High Level Committee, New Delhi.

Government of India. (2012), National synthesis report-Inclusion and exclusion of students in the school and in the classroom in primary and upper primary schools: A qualitative study commissioned by Sarva Shiksha Abhiyan, New Delhi.

Government of India. (1992), National policy on education 1986. New Delhi. MHRD, Department of Education.

Husain, S. (2010), Educational attainment of Muslim Women in India: Obstacles and Interventions. In A. Waheed (Ed.), *Minority Education in India: Issues of Access, Equity and Inclusion*. New Delhi, Serial Publications.

Jean Dreze and Amartya Sen (2006), *India, Development and Participation*, New Delhi, Oxford University Press.

Jha, J. (2005), Education of Muslims in India: An exploration in the issues of exclusion in plural society. Paper presented at the Oxford Conference on Education and Development, September, UK, Oxford

Jha, J., and D. Jhingran (2005), *Elementary education for the poorest and other deprived groups: The real challenge of universalisation.* New Delhi, Manohar.

Ministry of Human Resource Development (2013), Report of the Standing Committee of the National Monitoring Committee for Minorities Education.

Mondal, S. R. (1989), "Human Resource Development, Observation on Muslims in India", *Occasional Paper, No. 3,* Deptt. of Sociology and Social Anthropology, University of North Bengal.

Narulla Syed and J.P. Nayak, (1971), *A Students' History of Education in India*, Macmillan Company of India.

Pandey, P.N. (1988), "Education and Social Mobility", *A Text with Reference to Scheduled Caste*: Delhi, Daya Publishing House.

Shariff, A., and Razzack, A. (2006), *Social Development Report.* New Delhi, Oxford University Press.

UNESCO (2011). 'Regional Report on Progress towards Education for All in Asian and the Pacific' (UNESCO, Bangkok, 2011).

Year Book on Human Rights for 1950, New York (1952).

Part-Two
Women Empowerment and Muslim Society

6

Right to Education–A Status of Muslim Women of India: Broken Promises

Swati Chakraborty

Introduction

Even though Islam emphasises the right and importance of education unequivocally, access to education for Muslim women has been deeply severed. The Prophet stated: "Whosoever follows a path to seek knowledge therein, Allah will make easy for him/ her a path to Paradise." Similarly, the Quran asks, "Are those who know and who do not know equal?" Great emphasis has been placed on education and no distinction is made between men and women. Muslim women have played an important and historic role as scholars and leaders in education. For instance, the princess Fatima Al-Fihri established the first degree-granting University in the world, University of Al Karaouine, in Morocco in 859 CE. And during the Ayyubid dynasty, the regent queen Dafiya Khatun built numerous *khanqas* (Sufi convents) and *Madrasas* (theological schools) in Damascus and Aleppo.

However, Muslim women face restrictions in accessing education that differ greatly from one region to another. For example, in Afghanistan there is a denial of adequate education for young girls and women. Repression of women is still prevalent in rural areas, where girls are forced into early marriage and denied basic education. Numerous schools for girls have been burned down and some girls have even been poisoned to death for daring to go to school. Unfortunately, 80 percent of Afghan women are illiterate and only 30 percent of girls have access to education. This is a sharp contrast to some universities in the United Arab Emirates that have a female population approaching 80 percent. Other factors, such as poverty and shortage of nearby schools, also impact girls' education, particularly in remote areas.

Yet, there are similar underlying challenges that Muslim women face in trying to receive education. One such example is the traditional patriarchal interpretation of qiwamah, the notion that men are guardians of Muslim women. Although the Quran stipulates that both men and women are protectors of one another, the concept of qiwamah has been used to justify various restrictions on women that in turn hinder Muslim women's education. For instance, limiting women's right to free movement is a great impediment to free and equal access to education. In various regions Muslim girls are also forced to marry at a very early age and thus kept at home instead of in the classroom. They are taught that their only role is that of a wife and of a mother and are discouraged from seeking educational and professional opportunities. Muslim women and their rights to education is one of the most hotly debated topics when it comes to the religion; from both sides, from within, and almost always from those who are less informed. In fact, girls outnumber boys at tertiary level and many women hold high positions in public and private offices. The plight for education is also highly competitive and in our pluralistic, multi-cultural, multi-faith country, all children, girls and boys (regardless of their religion or race), are encouraged to study hard in school and do well at university level in order to be successful. Gender inequality is a common accusation made against Islam and a disparity in educational opportunities between men and women in many Muslim countries is often cited as a primary example of this. Education is seen as one of the pivotal factors in determining the economic, social and political advancement of a society and if, those making up over fifty percent of that society, are denied such a basic fundamental right then needless to say human rights activists will seek to find reasons for this disparity. Religion, particularly Islam is cited as a major stumbling block for women's advancement. Studies have shown that in many parts of Africa and South East Asia women's acquisition of knowledge is fervently opposed; regulated to secondary importance as compared to men or encumbered with so many restrictions as to make it almost impossible for female students to acquire a decent standard of education.

This is a sad reflection upon Muslims and the societies that we have built since knowledge is one of the important pillars upon which the edifice of Islam has been raised. The very fact that the first revelation upon the Holy Prophet (blessings and peace be upon him) contained the commandment to 'read' speaks volumes of the emphasis Islam lays on education. Within Islam there is no disagreement found on acquisition of knowledge being binding and obligatory. The importance and excellence of knowledge has been highlighted both directly and indirectly in over five hundred places in the Holy Qur'an.

Right to Education : Indian Scenario

Muslim women in India are a disadvantaged group often marginalised in scholarly literature and policy interventions. Over the past few decades, researchers, international agencies, and the Indian Government have paid particular attention to gender issues in India, however, explicitly and implicitly these issues tend to focus primarily on Hindu women. This occurs in large part because Hindus are the majority in India. Researchers focus on Hindu women because it is necessary to bring to light the patriarchal obstacles facing the majority of women in India. In addition, individuals in positions to conduct scholarly research or frame policy interventions tend to overwhelmingly be Hindu, contributing to the bias towards research on Hindu women. As a result, less is known about the experience of Muslim women in India. Recently, there has been an increasing interest in the issues Muslims face, as illustrated by the recent publication of The Social, Economic, and Educational Status of the Muslim Community of India: a Report, commissioned by the Indian Prime Minister to address the dearth of information regarding Muslims in India. However, literature on Muslims is still in its infancy and often looks at all Muslims, grouping Muslim men and women together. While some scholars have made considerable inroads in research on Indian Muslim women, few studies contain a comprehensive framework centering on the interplay of religion and gender on Muslim women, and virtually none focus on how these relationships have been modified by historical forces. Moreover, little research has empirically examined the effect of these forces on Muslim women's lives.

Primary aim of this paper is to contribute to this embryonic literature on Indian Muslim women, focusing on changes in education and employment over the last two decades of the twentieth century. Over the past thirty years, India has experienced tremendous social, political, and economic change. Many of these changes have been salient to Muslim women's lives. This dissertation argues that three factors have influenced their experience: modernising forces, religious discrimination and disadvantage, and the intricate relationship between the rise of Hindu fundamentalism and the Muslim community's response to this threat. Modernisation is a process, which involves economic growth, urbanisation, and industrialisation. For developing countries, it also entails the diffusion of Western ideas and systems. Modernisation causes immense transformations in societies such as changes in education, employment, gender roles and ideologies. While these changes are not always positive, particularly for women, this dissertation argues that modernisation has expanded education and employment opportunities for Hindu and Muslim men and women. However, for Muslim men and women, modernising forces are often moderated by historical disadvantage and religious discrimination.

Historically, occupational and educational mobility in India has been limited. Influenced by an occupationally based caste system, individuals have been generally expected to remain in the same social and economic position as their parents and ancestors. While this is changing for some disadvantaged groups, particularly Scheduled Castes and Scheduled Tribes, who benefit from affirmative action programmes in public employment and education, Muslims are generally not afforded this assistance despite the disadvantages they face. The disadvantage Muslims have experienced in the past and continue to experience is in part a product of religious discrimination. Muslims face considerable discrimination in both employment and education. Evidence also suggests that discrimination against Muslims is increasing. This dissertation argues that Muslim men and women have lower levels of wage employment and education because of past and current disadvantage and discrimination. Moreover, this disadvantage may have intensified in recent decades due to increased communal tensions. India has been experiencing a deepening religious divide and a rise in Hindu fundamentalism resulting in an increasingly defensive response from the Muslim community.

This may have a unique influence on Indian Muslim women and also Island Muslim women. When minority groups are threatened or attempt to gain previously denied social, political, and economic resources, they often try to create unity among group members. Various literatures argue that there are often negative implications for women within these communities, particularly among groups defining their identity in religious terms. However, literature discussing these issues primarily emerges from the field of cultural studies and tends to lack an empirical basis. The impact of these forces on women's day to day experiences in such areas as education and employment consequently have received little attention. This dissertation makes a unique contribution to the literature by empirically analysing changes in gender disparities in education and employment among Muslims, and by comparing them to similar changes among Hindus, in an era during which the rise of Hindu fundamentalism and the Muslim community's response to it has dominated the lives of Muslim men and women.

Since Independence, education of girls has been an area of national concern. The Constitution of India intended to assure Muslims and other Minorities equality of status and opportunities with other citizens to accelerate the process of educational and socio-economic justice. The Constitution of India grants the right to Equality and Right to Freedom of Religion and Protection of Interests of Minorities in regard to educational rights. A number of constitutional provisions exist for protection and promotion of the interests of these minority groups. Article 29 (1) and (2) of the Constitution grant citizens residing in the territory of India or any part thereof having a distinct language, script of culture of its own shall have the right to conserve the same and no citizen shall be denied admission into any educational institution maintained by the State or receiving aid out of State funds on grounds only of religion, race, caste, language or any of them. Article 30 (1) and (2) grants right to all minorities, whether based on religion or language, to establish and administer educational institutions of their choice and the State shall not, in granting aid to educational institutions, discriminate against any educational institution on the ground that it is under the management of a minority, whether based on religion or language. Article 1 (350). A states it shall be the endeavour of every State and every local authority within the State to provide adequate facilities for instruction in the mother-tongue at the primary stage of education to children belonging to linguistic minority groups; and the President of India may issue such directions to any State as he/she considers necessary or proper for securing the provision of such facilities.

After attaining independence, efforts have been made to Universalisation of Elementary Education (UEE) in pursuance of Article 45 of the Constitution of India. Various strategies have been developed to broaden the base of access to elementary education. A number of Educations for All programmes have been launched to ensure enrolment and retention of children at the elementary stage. Consequently, number of schools has been increased and enrolments have been increased. The overall literacy rates have gone up from 18.33 percent in 1950-51 to 62 percent in 2001. Female literacy rate has also shown a considerable increase and also gone up from 8.86 percent in 1950-51 to 54 percent in 2001. However, there still exists a considerable disparity between the male and female literacy rates. The intra female literacy disparity continues to be high, the rural female, the socially disadvantaged groups (SCs and STs) and certain minorities are at the bottom of the ladder. However, during the last five decades, the trend of upward mobility is noticed among Scheduled Castes and Scheduled Tribes because of special treatment given to them through reservations, provisions for various incentive schemes, opening of residential schools and more access to government jobs etc. Certain minorities feel that they are deprived of such advantages and are lagging behind in all aspects of life as compared to the majority groups. In case of minorities although the census does enlist their population yet no further information is given about their educational status. It is a fact that the census collects information about all communities but no data is compiled and published beyond giving the religion-wise break up of population figures.

Some data that is compiled and retained in the records is treated as classified and is not available for use. It is, therefore, only on the basis of observations and sample studies that broad inferences can be drawn on the educational status of minorities in the absence of hard data. The findings of earlier research studies show that Muslims are comparatively educationally backward minority community as compared to other minority communities. With a total population of 838, 583, 988, Hindus accounted for 687, 646, 721 (82%) ; Muslims 101, 596, 057 (12.12%) ; Christians 19, 640, 284 (2.34%) ; Sikhs 16, 259, 744 (1.94%) ; Buddhists 6, 387, 500 (0.76%) ; Jains 3, 352, 706 (0.34%) ; other religions and persuasions 3, 369, 355 (0.39%) and 415.569 (0.04%) are from religion not stated (Census of India, 1991). There are a number of districts in the country where concentration of Muslim population is very high. In some districts their proportion ranges between 20 percent and 60 percent of the total population. There are other areas where the Muslim population is not visible and they are living for ages in the midst of Hindus and bound together in cultural and social practices.

Educational Development of Muslim Girls in the Pre-Independence Period

At the beginning of the 19th century educational facilities for women in the indigenous system of learning (*Tols, Pathshalas, Maktabs,* and *Madrasas*) were virtually non-existent as per the available literature. The social status of women was low and women of the middle and upper classes led a life of seclusion under the dominance of family males and interaction with non-family males was prohibited. Among upper class Muslims families girls were taught only to read the Quran in Arabic and incidentally to read Urdu and Persian. Many parents disallowed their daughters to go to schools as this was considered violation of the Islamic rules. The struggle for formal education of Muslim women began at the end of nineteenth century. Sir Mulana Hali and Sheikh Abdullah took the lead to fight for the cause of education for Muslim women. Sir Hali started a small primary school in 1894 for the daughters of his family and friends in Panipat. Unfortunately, the school had to close down after a few years due to the non-availability of female teacher for the school. For the first time in 1896, a resolution was placed by Khwaja Ghulamus in annual session of Muslim Education Conference for giving some attention to the education of Muslim women.

A women's bench was set up and Murtaza Ali was appointed as Secretary of this bench. In 1902, Sheikh Abdullah became the Secretary of the women's bench at the annual session of the Muslim Education Conference in Delhi. At that point of time the general perception of the leading personalities was that there should be a normal school for training of women teachers so that they can teach Muslim girls of high class families in their homes. Sir Sheikh Abdullah did not agree with the view because his perception was that there had to be a sufficient number of middle passed Muslim girls first and then only they could be trained as teachers. Sultan Jehan, the Begum of Bhopal was the first women in the Indian history who believed in the emancipation of women through education. She started the first school for Muslim girls in 1903 the Sultania School. There were 140 girls below 10 years of age in the school in the very first year. The complete transport arrangements were made to bring girls to schools and back to home. They were taught subjects-Urdu, English, Arithmetic, Geography and Domestic Economics. However, emphasis was more on religious education. Education of girls and women has transited from extreme opposition to total acceptance by the end of the last century. In 1904, Sheikh Abdullah started bringing out a monthly magazine, Khatoon, to popularise the idea of a school for Muslim girls in Aligarh. The Begum of Bhopal, Sultan Jehan immediately started giving regular grants to the girl's school in Aligarh. She promised to give annual grant of Rupees 1, 200 for the school. Fortunately, a resolution was passed in the annual Muslim Education Conference session at Lucknow to establish a girl's school in Aligarh and the school was opened in 1906. In the beginning there were only six girls in the school. In 1911, Sakhawat Memorial Girls High School was started in Bengal by Rokeya Sakhawat Hussain. Maulana Karamat Hussain and the Raja of Mahmudabad also supported for girl's education and started a girl's school in Lucknow in 1912.

Governmental Efforts to Promote Education of Minorities

Since Independence, the Government of India has appointed various Committees and Commissions to look into the problems of education of all children. Several policies are being formulated to promote and strengthen education of children. With regard to education of Minorities, some of the important recommendations are discussed below. The Report of the Education Commission (1964-66) embodies the principles of the Constitution and applies them specifically to educational opportunity: a society that values social justice and is anxious to improve the lot of the common men and cultivate all available talent; must ensure progressive equality of opportunity to all sections of the population. This is the only guarantee for building up of an egalitarian and human society in which the exploitation of the weak will be minimised.

The National Policy on Education (1979) recommends that as per positive efforts should be taken to promote the educational interest of the minorities which will help to protect the rights of minorities which was discussed during the Conference of

Chief Ministries of States and Central Ministry (National Policy on Education, Ministry of Education and Social Welfare, GOI, 1974, pp. 8-9). The National Policy on Education 1979 states "The country is conscious of the important contribution of the country's composite culture that can be made by organisations run by linguistic and religious minorities and admit and with right to establish such educational institutions of their choice and administer them in accordance with law, in order that the goal of an integrated Indian Community is achieved" (NPE 1979, Ministry of Education and Social Welfare, GOI, p. 21).

In 1983, Smt. Indira Gandhi, the then Prime Minister of India had issued 15 point programme for the welfare of Minorities.

- Point 11 directs the State authorities to take steps for starting of coaching classes in minority educational institutions to train minority students to compete successfully in admission and recruitment tests.
- Point 12 directs the States to make arrangement to set up ITIs and Community Polytechnics by Government or Private Agencies in predominantly minority areas to encourage admission in these institutions of persons belonging to the minority communities.

Policy Focus and Implementation Strategies to Promote Education of Backward Communities

The National Policy on Education (NPE) 1986 revised in 1992 and its Programme of Action (POA), envisages paying greater attention to the education of the educationally backward minorities in the interest of equality and social justice. The NPE 1986 and revised in 1992 states "Some minority groups are educationally deprived or backward. Greater attention will be paid to the education of these groups in the interest of equality and social justice. This will naturally include the Constitutional guarantees given to them to establish and administer their own educational institutions, and protection to their languages and culture." On the basis of 1981 Census data on literacy, it was found that there are a number of districts where literacy rates are extremely low in general and particularly among the females. It was further observed that a majority of these districts had substantial populations of Muslims. Even in States which are educationally very forward e.g. Kerala, the Muslim dominated districts were comparatively found educationally backward. The POA 1986 identified 41 educationally backward districts having sizeable population of Muslims and also spell out the following measures with the strategies recommended in addition to the on-going programmes of Education Department for improving the educational status of children belonging to such minority groups in general and of minority girls in particular.

Women's Education with Regard to Backward Minorities

As the women literacy and the girls' enrolment is lowest among educationally backward minorities, in the schemes of opening of girls schools, appointment of lady teachers, opening of girl's hostels and providing of incentives in the form of mid-day meals, uniforms etc. minorities' needs should be fully met.

Table 6.1: Distribution of Literacy Rate of Muslims (2001)

Rural			Urban		
Total	**Male**	**Female**	**Total**	**Male**	**Female**
53	62	43	70	76	63

Source: Sachar Committee Report 2006.

The Sachar Committee has brought out the backwardness faced by the Muslims through various other indicators. In almost every three Muslim-dominated villages, one does not have a school. Nearly 40 percent of the Muslim-dominated villages do not have any health facility. Worker population ratios for Muslims are significantly lower in rural areas, and marginally lower in urban areas. The lower ratios are mainly due to much lower participation in economic activity by Muslim women.

Status of Muslim Women: Educational Development

Education is an indispensable means for helping the Muslim women out of their economic misery because economic dependency is the major factor contributing to the low status of Muslim women. After independence women's education made considerable progress in India. The number of girl's schools and colleges increased. Muslim girls going to schools and colleges also increased slowly but steadily. Muslim parents are becoming anxious to educate their daughters along with their sons.

Village girls are going to schools while in towns many of them are seeking higher education. Still Muslim women are changing very gradually. Sometimes; the change is painfully slow, because for a long time Muslim women have remained secluded and have lived the life of submission, so most of them dislike the idea of change. Participation of Muslim girls in educational activities has been studied by Hassan and Menon (2004) who found that very few Muslim women in India are in high profile jobs. The study reveals that less than 15 percent of Muslim women report themselves to be working. Generally, Muslim women are self-employed or engaged in home-based labour. This leads to a huge dropout of Muslim girls from schools. The Sachar Committee Report (2006) also reflects the same feeling that parents feel that education is not important for girls. Even if girls are enrolled, they are withdrawn at an early age to marry them off. This leads to a higher dropout rate among Muslim girls. At the all India level Muslim women are three times behind their Hindu sisters. The attainment of higher education among girls is a rare phenomenon ever in the urban areas. The studies done in the field of Muslim women revealed that the lack of good quality schools and hostel facilities for girls, poor quality of teacher are believed to be some of the important factors responsible for the low level of educational attainment among Muslims women. It is worthwhile to say that Muslim women has a strong desire and enthusiasm for education, but hurdles like low access to schools in the vicinity, poverty, financial constraints and discrimination faced at school prevent them from continuing education.

Determination is an element without which no person can succeed in any venture. Muslim women should create will power or determination towards education so that they can reach to a peak of elevation. Due to the influence of ancient traditions and practices in Muslim societies especially in remote areas women loose courage from the childhood and become dependent on man, Parents also discourage their female children for higher studies. Muslim women suffer more because they are not given enough freedom and hardly have access to higher education, though even the primary level education is not easily accessible to them. There is also lack of schools and colleges in the areas where there is a higher concentration of the Muslim population. Girls are enrolled in nearby schools and are not sent far off to study due to safety reasons. Therefore, the Muslim women of the day need to develop their capabilities and making them more confident. These all demand a thorough discussion among policy-makers, academician and community leaders.

Table 6.2: Children Currently Studying as a Proportion of Population by Age-groups (2004-05)

Age-group (in Years)	Muslim Percentage
6-13	14.0(15.1)
14-15	12.2(14.5)
16-17	10.7(14.0)
18-22	10.2(13.9)
23 and above	7.4(10.9)

Source: Sachar Committee Report, Figures in parentheses show the proportion of the community in the respective age-group.

Concerns of Muslim Women's Education in India

Indian culture is distinct in nature where each ethnic group has the liberty to maintain their Religious identity. Muslim society of India is very heterogeneous in nature mainly because of the influence of caste system; Muslims are among most backwards in India. They are not taking care of their educational advancement by the advantage of constitutional provision. The problem of backwardness is a long term process. Muslims are far lagging behind than the other communities in terms of economically, socially, educationally as well as politically. There are various reasons for Muslim being educationally backward which are:

- The anti-Muslim attitude taken by British before independence to curtail the educational and employment opportunities of the community has laid a drastic impact on their socio-economic condition. The Muslims are facing the same problem even today. This attitude towards Muslims has pushed them in more backwardness.
- The Riots, communal violence and insecurity, have become the norm and a sad reality in Modern India. The majority of the victims of riots in India are Muslims. This situation is affecting their economic as well as social condition.
- Muslims are facing socio-economic poverty from past. Their vision is blurring towards education because majority of Muslim parents are illiterate, they are unaware about the importance of modern education. They live in large family size and give greater importance to early marriages. There is absent of vocational education to improve their image to develop through education.
- There is negative attitude towards girl's education among Muslims. Due to hurdles from family they lose the zeal to achieve something through education and thus they themselves do not have academic interest. If at all they are fortunate enough to go to a good school, they are often discouraged to go for higher education, especially overseas. There is often misconception regarding the "purity" of girls if they have studied in Universities, or have traveled abroad. The most important reason is that there is difficulty in finding educated groom if the girl becomes highly educated.
- As identified by Sachar Committee that normally Muslim Settlements are systematically deprived of access to infrastructure and public services, like power, piped water supplies and sewerage. Muslim community is living in low income, filthy and poor living conditions.

- Muslims are having poor facilities in their schools as well as proper education is also absent. Most of the schools are traditional, having problem of medium. The education is also not linked with employment opportunities.
- *Madarsa* and *Maktabs* are still running at the traditional pattern. There is no influence of modern education in their syllabus. Students of *Madarsa* are having low level of knowledge regarding commerce and computer etc.
- There is absence of committed and genuine Muslim leadership (both social and political) in pre- and post-independent India.

Conclusion

While the Covenant provides for progressive realisation and acknowledges the constraints due to the limits of available resources, it also imposes on States parties various obligations which are of immediate effect. 19 States parties have immediate obligations in relation to the right to education, such as the "guarantee" that the right "will be exercised without discrimination of any kind" [Art. 2 (2)] and the obligation "to take steps" [Art. 2 (1)] towards the full realisation of article 13. Such steps must be "deliberate, concrete and targeted" towards the full realisation of the right to education. The realisation of the right to education over time, that is "progressively", should not be interpreted as depriving States parties' obligations of all meaningful content. Progressive realisation means that States parties have a specific and continuing obligation "to move as expeditiously and effectively as possible" towards the full realisation of article 13.There is a strong presumption of impermissibility of any retrogressive measures taken in relation to the right to education, as well as other rights enunciated in the Covenant. If any deliberately retrogressive measures are taken, the State party has the burden of proving that they have been introduced after the most careful consideration of all alternatives and that they are fully justified by reference to the totality of the rights provided for in the Covenant and in the context of the full use of the State party's maximum available resources.

The Right to Education, like all human rights, imposes three types or levels of obligations on States parties: the obligations to respect, protect and fulfil. In turn, the obligation to fulfil incorporates both an obligation to facilitate and an obligation to provide. The obligation to respect requires States parties to avoid measures that hinder or prevent the enjoyment of the right to education. The obligation to respect requires States parties to take measures that prevent third parties from interfering with the enjoyment of the right to education. The obligation to fulfil (facilitate) requires States to take positive measures that enable and assist individuals and communities to enjoy the right to education. Finally, States parties have an obligation to fulfil (provide) the right to education. As a general rule, States parties are obliged to fulfil (provide) a specific right in the Covenant when an individual or group is unable, for reasons beyond their control, to realise the right themselves by the means at their disposal. However, the extent of this obligation is always subject to the text of the Covenant.

It is thus imperative, if a nation wishes to be successful and move towards a sustainable reality, the women of that society must be given every opportunity to attain knowledge and education which is not only her due but a right that has been ordained to her by Almighty.

REFERENCES

Ansari, A. I., (1989), "Muslim Educational Backwardness", in Iqbal A. Ansari (ed.) *The Muslim Situation in India*, New Delhi, Sterling Publishers Pvt. Ltd.

Chauhan, C.P.S. (2012), Participation of Indian Muslims in Educative Process, in Mirza Asmer Beg and A.R. Kidwai (ed.) *Empowerment of Indian Muslims, Perspective, Planning and Road Ahead*, New Delhi, Concept Publishing Company.

Fahimuddin, (2004), *Modernisation of Muslim Education in India*, Delhi, Adhyayan Publishers and Distributors.

Gupta, S., (2012) The Education of Muslims in India, *All International Research Journal,* Vol. III, Issue-35.

Hamid, S., (1985), "Educational Status of Indian Muslims" *Muslim India*.

Khan, M. A., (1984) *Muslims in the Process of Rural Development in India*, New Delhi, Uppal Publishing House.

Mondal, S. R., (1989), "Human Resource Development, Observation on Muslims in India", *Occasional Paper,* No. 3, Deptt. of Sociology and Social Anthropology, University of North Bengal.

Nasrin, (2013), Education of Muslim Women, A Journey from Past to Present, *International Journal of Management and Social Sciences, Research*, Volume 2, No. 1.

National Policy on Education, Ministry of Education and Social Welfare, GOI, 1974.

Phadke, Y. D. (1978), Education of Muslims and schedule caste since independence, *Lala Lajpat Rai Memorial Lectures*, 1977-78, Bombay: Lala Lajpatrai Institute.

Premi, Mahendra K. (2006), *Population of India in the New Millenium: Census 2001*, New Delhi, National Book Trust.

Siddiqui, M. H. (2012), Educational Backwardness of Muslims in India and its Possible Remedies, *Indian Journal of Applied Research*, Volume 2, Issue-3.

Talib, P., (2012), Educational Initiatives to transform Muslim Community, in Mirza Asmer Beg and A.R. Kidwai (ed.), *Employment of Indian Muslims, Perspective, Planning and Road Ahead,* New Delhi, Concept Publishing House.

7

State, Religion and the Issues of Empowerment :The Status of Muslim Women in India

K.M. Sajad Ibrahim

The case of Muslim women deserves special attention given the fact that they are one of the most vulnerable sections in India. In all religions, the status of women is inferior to that of men. However, women have the possibilities to come out of the male dominated system and to explore their own development. In the case of Islam, it has given a most dignified position to women than any other religions in the world. Unfortunately, this dictum never been practised in the case of Muslim women, especially in India. In north India, they are the victims of different types of atrocities like riots, isolation, injustice, violence etc. This situation directly affected the status of Muslim women, and their role was confined within the domestic matters of their families. Here, the question focuses on the role of Islam, and the current Indian scenario, which thwart Muslim women empowerment.

Status of Women in Islam

Islam has bestowed highest status to women. This is visible from the texts of Quran and teachings of Prophet Muhammed.

The Quran provides clear-cut evidence that woman is completely equated with man in the sight of God in terms of her rights and responsibilities. The Quran states: "Every soul will be (held) in pledge for its deeds" [Noble Quran 74:38]

It also states: "...So their Lord accepted their prayers, (saying) : I will not suffer to be lost the work of any of you whether male or female. You precede one from another..." [Noble Quran 3:195]

Woman according to the Quran is not blamed for Adam's first mistake. Both were jointly wrong in their disobedience to God, both repented, and both were forgiven. [Noble Quran 2:36, 7:20-24]

With regard to the woman's right to seek job it should be stated first that Islam regards her role in society as a mother and a wife as the most sacred and essential one. Neither maids nor baby-sitters can possibly take the mother's place as the educator of an upright, complex free, and carefully-reared children. Such a noble and vital role, which largely shapes the future of nations, cannot be regarded as "idleness".

However, there is no decree in Islam, which forbids woman from seeking employment whenever there is a necessity for it, especially in positions, which fit her nature, and in which society needs her most. Examples of these professions are nursing, teaching (especially for children), and medicine. Moreover, there is no restriction on benefiting from woman's exceptional talent in any field. Even for the position of a judge, where there may be a tendency to doubt woman's fitness for the post due to her more emotional nature, we find early Muslim scholars such as Abu-Hanifah and At-Tabari holding there is nothing wrong with it. In addition, Islam restored to woman the right of inheritance, after she herself was an object of inheritance in some cultures. Her share is completely hers and no one can make any claim on it, including her father and her husband.

According to Islam, men and women are moral equals in God's sight and are expected to fulfil the same duties of worship, prayer, faith, alms giving, fasting, and pilgrimage to Mecca. Islam brought considerable improvement in the status of women compared to earlier Arab cultures, prohibiting female infanticide and recognising women's full personhood. Islamic law emphasises the contractual nature of marriage, requiring that a dowry be paid to the woman rather than to her family, and guaranteeing women's rights of inheritance and to own and manage property. Moreover, women were granted the right to live in the matrimonial home and receive financial maintenance during marriage and a waiting period following death and divorce.

There were several historical records, which show that Muhammad consulted women and weighed their opinions seriously. Women prayed in mosques un-segregated from men, were involved in *hadith* transmission, gave sanctuary to men, engaged in commercial transactions, were encouraged to seek knowledge, and were both instructors and pupils in the early Islamic period. Muhammad's last wife, Aisha, was a well-known authority in medicine, history, and rhetoric.

No woman held religious titles in Islam, but many women held political power, some jointly with their husbands, others independently.[1] In the west, the common picture of a Muslim woman is the stereotype of a woman hidden behind a veil, a voiceless, silent figure, bereft of rights. It is a picture familiar to all of us, in large part because this is invariably how the western media portrays women in Islam. Islam covers many lands with many diverse cultures. From the borders of Arabia to the coasts of Africa, from Bosnia to Indonesia, large groups of people practice Islam. Islam is growing in European and American countries. Each one of these Islamic nations has its own distinct culture; there is a great diversity of cultures within Islam. One cannot bring all these cultures, political systems, national heritage, belief systems, geographical locations, historical backgrounds, and the peoples who embody them under one uniform category or think of them as one system. Islam is practiced in each nation according to those nations' characteristics. In addition, nations are, by existing as nations, distinct and different from one another. No two cultures are alike.

"Paradise lies under the feet of mothers", declared the Prophet. With this instruction, a Divine Law, it became a religious responsibility, a praiseworthy act, to respect and honour women. "Men are support for women," "Among the praiseworthy acts to Allah is to treat your mother with honour and respect, " "Be just among your children, daughters and sons, provide them good education and proper upbringing." Narrated from the Prophet (swa): "with these Divine laws, it became religious duty for every Muslim, male or female, to honour women, treat sons and daughters justly, and for male to provide support, not obstacles, for women and their achievements."

Shushtery (1938) comments that Islam contributed to the status improvement of women in the following ways: (i) By stressing the need to respect and to give good treatment to a foster mother, (ii) By entrusting women with the status of mistress of her own property in which the husband had no right to interfere except with her permission, (iii) By giving her the right of claiming divorce (Khula), (iv) By allowing her to hold any public office, (v) By giving her the freedom to remarry after divorce, and (vi) By encouraging her to study and acquire knowledge.

Kapadia (1965) writes that Islam improved the status of women through different means. It includes by restricting polygamy to four wives and favouring monogamy, by condemning female infanticide, by assigning share in inheritance, by declaring Mehr as a compulsory gift to the bride and by re-orienting the Arab law of marriage and divorce in favour of women like providing maintenance (for iddat period) for divorced women and their children. Paradise was promised to a believing woman as it was to a believing man.

In Islam, ignorance is an unforgivable sin, so is your evasion of responsibility for yourself as well as towards all the members of the living world, past and present. It is incorrect to blame such Islam for the shortcomings of its followers, which are the failings of most of mankind. A religion that is centered on the rights of human being, and sets both men and women free from the chains of bondage should not be used in propaganda for the sake of condemnation. It is not Muslim women as such, but women everywhere who have been imprisoned by prejudice and cruelty. This form of prejudice that goes beyond simple racial or national boundaries is sexual in nature. Whether women are constantly being held to an impossible standard or subject to discrimination solely because they are not equal to men, they are, by far, the group most affected by this form of prejudice. Depending on the society, women may be seen as having the wrong weight, the wrong height, the wrong level of intelligence, or the wrong religion. We can conclude that women have yet to be welcomed with open arms into countries that they have been a part of from the beginning.

Muslim Women in India

The status of women in Indian society is a much-debated subject. There are points of view put forth defending or condemning the position occupied by or imposed upon women in the Indian subcontinent. The position of women under Islam has been the subject of repeated controversies among educated Muslims ever since they came under the impact of Western liberalisation. The controversial subject of women's rights has assumed great importance in the Islamic world and is a burning issue today.

Muslim females in India number more than 71 million (over seven percent of the population) (Census of India, 2011), and are disadvantaged thrice over in Indian society: as women, as members of a minority community, and as individuals in poverty. Sixty percent of Muslim women are married before the legal age of 18, over 50 percent are illiterate and over 75 percent report that they need permission from their husbands for virtually every activity related to their personal, social, familial or health concerns (Hasan and Menon, 2004. pp. 76-77, 237). Many do not realise they have rights, or that their own religion accords them rights. They are not connected to other women in an empowering framework. They live in a cycle that is difficult to break: poverty and isolation leads to poor health and education, which are barriers in gaining the skills and knowledge necessary to emerge from poverty. The isolation of the Muslim community, along with its attitudes to education, has affected the ability of Muslim women in India to be represented in mainstream public life. In recent years only two Muslim women were members of the Indian Parliament (Rai, 2002, p. 3) out of a total 790 seats (i.e. less than half a percent). The ghettoisation of Muslims has deprived them further of Government infrastructure such as schools, roads, garbage disposal and sewerage facilities and health centres (Action Aid, 2006, p. 5). While affirmative action programmes for deprived groups exist in India, historically this has not extended to Muslims, and this is one of the reasons for the lack of progress in education for Muslims (de Haan, 2011, p. 17).

Even after six decades of independence majority of Muslim women are disadvantaged, least literate, economically impoverished and politically marginalised sections of Indian society. Despite the claim that Quran bestows equal status and rights on both men and women, the reality is different. In Muslim society in India, the Muslim women have lower status than their men have and do not enjoy equal rights both in the family and outside.

One important reason is that the Muslims in India are among the most marginalised communities. In this context, two important factors have thwarted the status of Muslim women in India. First, it was contributed by the religious orthodoxy of patriarchal society, and secondly, the neglect of the state on matters related to such vulnerable sections. Both men and women have equal role in the development process of a society, especially in a developing country like India. Hence, modernisation and development are inevitable to improve the inferior status of Muslim women. Moreover, the liberation of women is a part of the development of a community. As such, Muslim women empowerment will be an answer to their current problems. Unfortunately, the religious taboos imposed by the community deny Muslim women any improvement of their status. For empowerment, education is an important requirement. However, Muslim women in most parts of north India have education only from *Madrasa*, and not from any formal institutions. As part of protecting the community identity Women are prevented from entering into public. As such, they are denied educational and employment opportunities. Three distinct opinions are being expressed on the status of Muslim women in India.

One opinion says that Islam and Islamic law have nothing to do with present disadvantaged status of Muslim women. This view stresses that the status of Muslim women is similar to that of other caste women in the country, the most important reason being poverty and illiteracy.

The second view is that Islam imposes many restrictions on its women and gives higher status to men and concentrates power in the hands of men.

The third view is that Islamic law treats both men and women as equals but unfortunately the Islamic scholars and religious leaders are misinterpreting the Islamic law giving men power over women.

Like other women, Muslim women too are not a monolithic community. There are women belonging to different sects, social groups, occupations, regional, linguistic-cultural groups, educational levels, etc. Their lives are similarly at the intersection of gender, family and community within the dynamic context of Indian society, polity and economy. Thus, Muslim women in India tend to suffer not just the disabilities attached to the female status, but also to the Muslim community's impoverished minority status in the country. Muslims form the largest minority community and the second largest religious group in India. Hence, there is a direct relation between the status of Muslims in India and the status of Muslim women.

However, the available literature on the condition of Muslims in India reveals that they are a backward minority. They are educationally most backward, economically poor and politically a powerless community in India. This fact of minority status of Muslims in India has been conclusively established in several reports and surveys of government and also by individual researchers.

The Ministry of Home Affairs in the early 1980s to enquire into the condition of religious minorities, Schedule Castes (SCs) and Schedule Tribes (STs) set up high Power Panel under the Chairmanship of Dr. Gopal Singh. The Committee's findings revealed that Muslims and Neo-Buddhists were the most educationally backward communities at the national level (Government of India, 1983, pp. 3&4). It was found that their economic condition was worse than those of Schedule Castes (SCs) and Schedule Tribes (STs). They were deprived of the benefits of developmental schemes and were underrepresented in governmental services and decision-making bodies (Zakaria, 1995, pp. 163-166).

In March 2005, Prime Minister Manmohan Singh appointed a High-level committee headed by Justice Rajinder Sachar to prepare a report on the social, economic and educational status of Indian Muslims. The report highlighted the deplorable socio-economic plight of the Muslim community in India. It notes that the community exhibits "deficits and deprivation" in practically all dimensions of development. "In fact, by and large, Muslims rank somewhat above SCs/STs but below Hindu OBCs, other Minorities and Hindu General (mostly upper castes) in almost all indicators considered" (Government of India, 2006, p. 237). The poor representation of Muslims in the employment market was also highlighted. A significantly large proportion of, Muslim workers are engaged in the informal sector of the economy with little or no social security and their participation in the formal sector employment is significantly less than the national average. In no state does the representation of Muslims in the Government departments match their population share. Muslims' presence in the private sector was found to be even more dismal. The Committee also found that the large proportion of community is with poor civic amenities and infrastructure facilities. In fact, the Muslims face high levels of poverty and their condition is only slightly better than that of SCs and STs (Government of India, 2006).

Many scholars have also pointed out the socio-economic backwardness of Muslims in India (Siddiqui, 1984; Mondal, 1985; Siddiqui, 1987; Ansari, 1992; Khalidi, 1995). Thus, Muslims' backwardness results in a sense of discrimination. What is important is not the fact of discrimination against Muslims but the feeling of discrimination among them (Mathur, 1992).

The status of Muslims directly affects the condition of Muslim women. Presently, in the changing Indian society the Muslim women try hard to get rid of the burden of gender, family and community by way of getting them educated (Menon, 1981, p. 25). The amalgam between minority identity and stereotyped judgment on the issues of Muslim women can be easily broken if they receive proper education and become conscious of their rights as well as their duties. Education is therefore, their dire and essential need.

A book by Zoya Hasan and Ritu Menon (2004) presents the results of a national survey covering around 10, 000 Muslim and Hindu women. One of the standard assumptions about Muslim women is that religion prevents them from getting access to education. It is certainly true that Muslim women are more likely to be illiterate than Hindu women (in the survey, 59 percent had never attended school and less than 10 percent had completed school). However, the study shows that this is essentially the result of low socio-economic status, rather than religion. Across the survey, among all communities and caste groups, financial constraints and gender bias dominate over other factors in determining levels of education. Indeed, in those regions where Muslims are better off (as in the south and to a lesser extent in the west), Muslim women also have higher levels of education.

However, two other features that are more specific to the Muslim community may have operated to devalue continuing education for girls. The first is that Muslim men also have very low educational attainment in general. The study found that 26 percent of educated Muslim women had illiterate husbands. This low male education level would create further pressures to impose ceilings on girls' education. In addition, the low age of marriage is a major inhibiting factor. At the national level, the mean age of marriage of Muslim girls is very low at 15.6 years, and in the rural north, it falls to an appalling 13.9 years.

State Intervention on the Status of Indian Muslims

Article 14 of the Constitution grants equality to all citizens without discrimination on grounds of caste, language or religion. All minorities enjoy equal rights in public employment under

Article 16. Under Articles 26, 27 and 28 of the Indian Constitution minorities have the right to manage their own religious affairs, are not compelled to attend state-funded religious institutions, and receive equal treatment for minority-managed institutions. Article 30 ensures the right of minorities to administer their own educational institutions. Article 249 of the Indian Constitution grants Backward Classes a right to preferential treatment in order to bring them up to par with the rest of the population.

Successive Governments, however, have not been committed to removing the structural inequalities, which perpetuate class, caste and gender differentials; rather their policies towards reservation have been politically motivated. In 1977, for example, the Uttar Pradesh Government declared 37 Hindu castes and 21 Muslim groups as 'Backward Classes', entitling them to preferential treatment in education and employment. The Government order was overturned by the High Court, which ruled that this was unconstitutional; since it included groups, whose economic status did not require special concessions. In 1987, the Muslim *Majlis-e-Mushawarat* demanded the extension of 'reservation for the Muslim community as a Backward Class in public service and higher education'. However, this would still not guarantee that the factors behind their disadvantaged position would be removed, or indeed that those most deserving of reservation would be able to benefit from it.

Since the dawn of independence, the Government of India dominated by the Aryan Brahmins, adopted discriminatory measures against the Muslims. India has lived over half a century under secular Constitution but its Muslim population remained isolated from its political mainstream. Political parties as well as Muslim leadership used each other for their self-seeking political and communal interest respectively at the cost of common Muslims, who remained educationally and economically backward.

India is a vocal advocate of secularism but nowhere else in the world secularism was so blatantly betrayed. The Central Government knifed secularism by covertly becoming a party to the demolition of the Babari Masjid. Similarly, Secularism was deserted by the Bombay Police by openly participating in the killing of thousands of Muslims in the aftermath of the demolition of the Babari Masjid. The jails of Bombay are still packed with scores of innocent Muslims rounded up in the wake of the blast (12 March, 1993) but not a single brute involved in the massacre of the Muslims was brought to book. Those who were held under the notorious Terrorist and Disruptive Activities Act (TADA) were 90 percent Muslims, although the Muslims constituted only over 12 percent of the total population of the country. The instances of how the Muslims have been made target of all kinds of discrimination and subject of perennial persecution are endless. These all have resulted in a process whereby the Indian Muslims are fast moving towards ruination culturally, educationally, economically, socially and politically.

In Gujarat, the worst religious violence directed against Muslims by Hindus took place in February and March 2002, leaving an estimated 2, 000 dead and 100, 000 displaced into refugee camps. The events in Gujarat from 27 February 2002 mark a turning point in contemporary Indian politics. These have profound consequences for the continuation of India as a multi-cultural, secular society, for survival of democracy, and for the unity and integrity of the country. There have been riots and pogroms in India before but the Gujarat carnage is exceptional. Widespread communal violence erupted following the burning in Godhra of the Sabarmati Express train, in which fifty-nine men, women, and children were killed. The incident had sparked some of the deadliest sectarian violence seen in India.

The incident of Hindutva mob attack on Mohammed Akhlaq's house and his cold-blooded murder in subsequent lynching on 28 September, 2015 was the latest attack against Muslims. As absurd as it sounds a person lost his life and his whole house and family shattered only because of the rumours that he ate and had preserved beef in refrigerator. Muslims believe that that the mob attacks on deceased Mohammed Akhlaq's was a pre-planned act with political motivation close to Assembly elections in Bihar. Hindutva ideologues that are running the ruling party BJP lost the mandate on development and now want to get back the old habits of instigation on communal lines against the Muslim community to polarise Hindu vote banks in the name of cow. This incident should not be seen in isolation, Attacks on Muslims near National Capital Territory of Delhi, from Gopalgarh riots in Rajasthan, Muzaffarnagar and Shamli riots in Uttar Pradesh, to Atali riots in Haryana, and now Dadri lynching near Greater Noida have shown one same disturbing pattern. These communal attacks resulted in creating fear psychosis among minority Muslims population near Capital Territory often leading to exodus of Muslims from the NCTD region.

Violent events of this kind are typically called "Hindu-Muslim riots". The term is misleading since there is evidence that the attacks on Muslims, their property and their religious freedom normally were planned and premeditated. The talk of "Hindu-Muslim riots", however, suggests that both sides are equally to blame. A brutal irony of the matter is that Muslims' reputation for suffering communal violence makes it easy to portray them as potential terrorists and terror sympathisers. Indeed, BJP leaders have admitted that pogroms serve the "consolidation of the Hindu-vote" and are meant to render the political participation of Muslims futile. While Prime Minister Narendra Modi likes to present himself as the champion of development, his subtext is always one of consolidating Hindu power. The opposition Congress is also morally responsible for such heinous crimes. When the UPA was in power, no serious attempt was taken to pass the Communal Violence, which could have prevented such communal incidents. Moreover, the soft Hindutva policy followed by the Congress Party on many occasions also encouraged attack against religious minorities.

Sachar Committee Report (2006) confirmed that by most development indicators, the Muslim community is lagging behind other religious groups of India. Dropout rates are also highest among Muslims and this seems to go up significantly after middle school. Higher secondary attainment levels are also among the lowest for Muslims. The committee had identified poverty to be the major barrier to education amongst Muslims as young children are expected to support their family rather than to study. Their nutritional status in terms of per capita calorie intake is also lower than that of the rest of the population. As we know, literacy is the first step in learning and knowledge building, and therefore, an essential indicator of human development. According to the Sachar Committee in almost every three Muslim-dominated villages, one does not have a school. Nearly 40 percent of the Muslim-dominated villages do not have any health facility. Worker population ratios for Muslims are significantly lower in rural areas, and marginally lower in urban areas. The lower ratios are mainly due to much lower participation in economic activity by Muslim women.

There have not been any major Government programmes to improve the material condition of Muslims. On the other hand, Governments have heeded calls from patriarchal, self-styled leaders of Muslims on "protecting Muslims' faith". Such action was largely symbolical and is supposed to allow Muslims to live according to the Holy Scriptures. Unfortunately, the approach also gives space to right-wing Hindus to target Muslims further for their "unequal treatment of women". The truth, however, is that Indian society in general is deeply patriarchal and no religious community treats women fairly. The Hindus are no exception.

Indian culture is distinct in nature where each ethnic group has the liberty to maintain their religious identity. Muslim society of India is very heterogeneous in nature mainly because of the influence of caste system; Muslims are among most backwards in India. They are not taking care of their educational advancement by the advantage of constitutional provision. The problem of backwardness is a long term process. Muslims are far lagging behind than the other communities more economically, socially, educationally as well as politically. There are various reasons for Muslims being educationally backward which are:

There is negative attitude towards girls'education among Muslims. Due to hurdles from family, they lose the zeal to achieve something through education and thus they themselves do not have academic interest. If at all they are fortunate enough to go to a good school, they are often discouraged to go for higher education.

As identified by Sachar Committee, normally Muslim Settlements are systematically deprived of access to infrastructure and public services like power, piped water supplies and sewerage. Muslim community is living in low income, filthy and poor living conditions.

1. Muslims are having poor facilities in their schools as well as proper education is also absent. Most of the schools are traditional, having problem of medium. The education is also not linked with employment opportunities.
2. *Madrasa* and *Maktabs* are still running at the traditional pattern. There is no influence of modern education in their syllabus. Students of *Madrasa* are having low level of knowledge regarding commerce and computer etc.
3. There is absence of committed and genuine Muslim leadership (both social and political) in Pre- and Post-Independent India.

Even the state is not keen on the issues related to the marginalisation of Muslim community. No serious attempt was taken by the state to consider the recommendations of Sachar Committee report. The venomous attitude of Sangh Parivar led groups against Sachar Committee Report further prevented the state from considering the measures to improve the status of the Muslim Community as well as Muslim women. It is a good sign that courts have begun to acquit individual Muslims who were accused of terrorism and detained without proof for years. Victims of violence in the 2013 riots in Uttar Pradesh have gone to court, and some other cases are proceeding in a slow but promising manner. Indian Muslims are increasingly articulating their sense of hurt at being treated as non-citizens in their own country. They are expressing their dissatisfaction at being placated with mere lip service to cultural rights as a minority. They are beginning to claim their rights as equal citizens of a democratic country.

Roadblocks in the Muslim Women Empowerment

Empowerment is viewed as means of creating a social

environment in which one can make decisions and make choices either individually or collectively for social transformation. It strengthens the innate ability by way of acquiring knowledge, power and experience (Schuler and Riley, 1996). The empowerment of Muslim Women is inextricably intertwined with religion, social and cultural taboos imposed by the Muslim male members, the status of Muslim community in India and the role of state.

The 2005 Government of India Sachar Report found that both civil society and Government blame the religious community for the position of Muslim women, rather than societal discrimination or faulty development policies (Sachar Committee Report, 2006. pp. 12-13). However, there has since been more evidence of political will to address development issues of Muslims, specifically Muslim women. In its Eleventh Five Year Plan for 2007-2012, the Indian Government's Planning Commission specifically recognised the "double deprivation" of Muslim women and recommended targeted interventions for Muslim women as a priority area of action (Government of India, Planning Commission, 2007, p. 20).

The impact of Muslim women's isolation in society is damaging Indian democracy. Without the full participation of women in social and governance structures, socio-economic development is severely depressed. Beyond this, with such a significant portion of the community marginalised, it becomes vulnerable to the growth of anti-national and extremist ideologies. At a relatively benign level, this can lead to a perception among the Muslim community that mainstream political processes and institutions are not delivering for the marginalised, and many can lose faith in mainstream structures and political processes. On a more malignant level, it can lead to extremist violence.

Analysts also argue that vote-bank politicking leads to Hindu-Muslim electoral polarisation and reinforces the marginalisation of Muslims. It has been suggested that this kind of vote bank mentality suits some Muslim leaders, allowing them and various middlemen to bargain with political parties on behalf of a collective vote while in reality Indian Muslims espouse a range of political opinions.

Vote-bank politicking is a threat to the plurality of the Indian political system and weakens the ability of Muslims to engage in the system in a meaningful way. This is particularly so for Muslim women given their weak status. Ultimately, this is a threat to democracy, as individuals feel disempowered from having an individual stake in the democratic process and access to Government services

In India, the discursive identity of Muslim women has always revolved around the tropes of personal laws, *triple talaq and purdah* (veiling). All these tropes have produced them as a homogenous as well as political category. National debates on the Shah Bano case, Imrana[2] and Gudiya[3] cases have not only reified their victimhood but also raised the need for Muslim personal law reform to protect women's rights in Islam. The issue of personal law reform is not a new issue in Islamic societies. Many countries like Egypt, Malaysia had opted for Muslim personal law reform to ensure gender justice. However, in India, the issue of Muslim personal law reform through Uniform Civil Code[4] has remained extremely sensitive to the community. It is perhaps due to the reason that discourses on personal laws are religious, and based on their minority identity. Any reform in personal laws has been perceived as a threat to Islamic tradition and practices.

Therefore, the socio-political and cultural meanings of *triple talaq, purdah* (veiling) and polygamy have never been from the patriarchal influence, which have always accorded Muslim women a subordinate position in society. Muslim women's identity has to be perceived through these socio-political and cultural practices, as mediated through discourses and the effects of power (Basu, 2010, p. 76). In India, the religious leadership has remained over-possessive about the rights of Muslim women in India. Misogynist interpretations of the Quran, different types of *fatwas* exhibit that religious orthodoxies not only show a power hierarchy but also give rise to "little traditions", which are products of our own time, space and context.

The Indian State for many times has ended up with a judgment call where: the dominant discourse on Muslim women's rights largely prevailed over the alternative sets of knowledge, which derives its inspirations from a more egalitarian and gender-based understanding of Islam. The Indian State has remained confused over: the discourse to endorse; dominant or subjugated; liberal or communitarian; Muslim women as citizens of the Indian state or the wards of community? Shah Bano, (a 65-year-old woman) filed a case against her husband and the Supreme Court granted her appeal for lifelong maintenance from her husband. In order to overcome the judgment, the orthodox elements of Islamic community approached the Government since they viewed this judgment as un-Islamic. As such, Rajiv Gandhi Government enacted the Muslim Women (Protection of Rights on Divorce) Bill, 1986. This bill explicitly excluded Muslim women from the right to maintenance available under the CrPC13 (Hasan, 2000, pp. 265-269). This attitude of Government is only to woo the orthodox elements of Muslim community as part of vote bank and least interested in the issues faced by the Muslim women. Of late, the Supreme Court has called for a reassessment of the Muslim Women Act, 1986, pointing out that India's Criminal Procedure Code, which applies to all citizens, provides maintenance to divorced women for their lifetime with the exception of remarriage. This was based on a hearing of a case in October 2015 related to the violation of Muslim women's right due to the discriminatory provisions in the Muslim personal law.

Conclusion

For Muslim women of India they have to face multiple obstructions to find empowerment. The first category is from the male dominated community leaders and family members, who distort Islam for their personal interest. Second category comes from the Sangh Parivar dominated Indian society who target Muslims for their political interest. As such, the Muslims had been the victims of different types of communal politics, especially from the Babari Masjid issue to the latest beef politics like Dadri lynching near Greater Noida. Finally, third category is the state, which is least interested in the matters of Muslims. Even if they take any appeasing action, it would be only for the interest of the Muslim men as happened in the case of Shah Bano case. In fact, their interest is only in the vote bank politics.

NOTES

1. The best-known women rulers in the pre-modern era include Khayzuran, who governed the Muslim Empire under three Abbasid caliphs in the eighth century; Malika Asma bint Shihab al-Sulayhiyya and Malika Arwa bint Ahmad al-Sulayhiyya, who both held power in Yemen in the eleventh century; Sitt al-Mulk, a Fatimid queen of Egypt in the eleventh century; the Berber queen Zaynab al-Nafzawiyah (r. 1061 – 1107) ; two thirteenth-century Mamluk queens, Shajar al-Durr in Cairo and Radiyyah in Delhi; six Mongol queens, including Kutlugh Khatun (thirteenth century) and her daughter Padishah Khatun of the Kutlugh-Khanid dynasty; the fifteenth-century Andalusian queen Aishah al-Hurra, known by the Spaniards as Sultana Madre de Boabdil; Sayyida al-Hurra, governor of Tetouán in Morocco (r. 1510-1542); and four seventeenth-century Indonesian queens.
2. .In 2005, a 70-year-old father-in-law raped a young girl named Imrana in a remote village of Uttar Pradesh. Religious leaders and the caste Panchayat issued the fatwa that she had to get married to her father-in-law, and consider her husband as her son. The Women's Commission and the State could not do anything on the ground that it was an internal affair of the community.
3. Gudiya's case came into media focus in August when Mohammad Arif, who had gone missing in action since the 1999 Kargil war, was repatriated by Pakistan as a Prisoner of War. During the five-year absence of Arif, who was presumed dead after initially being declared a deserter, Gudiya had married Taufiq and carried his child. After his marriage, Arif had spent a very short time with Gudiya, as he was called for service during the Kargil conflict. On his return to his native village, Arif found his wife Gudiya married to Taufiq. However, the village council reunited Arif and Gudiya following a decision. Taufiq, who hails from Pataudi village in Gurgaon, tried to get Gudiya back but the council ruled in favour of Arif and, she had since then been living with him (Kumar, 2006: 1).
4. Uniform Civil Code in India is the debate to replace the personal laws based on the scriptures and customs of each major religious community in the country with a common set governing every citizen. These laws are distinguished from public law and cover marriage, divorce, inheritance, adoption and maintenance. Article 44 of the Directive Principles of State Policy set its implementation as duty of the State. Apart from being an important issue regarding secularism in India, and it became one of the most controversial topics in contemporary politics during the Shah Bano case in 1985. The debate then focused

on the Muslim Personal Law, which is partially based on the Sharia law and remains unreformed since 1937, permitting unilateral divorce and polygamy in the country (Hasan, 2000).

REFERENCES

Action Aid, Jahangirabad (2006), Media Institute and Indian Social Institute, Preliminary Report on the Socio-Economic Condition of the Muslims in India <http://www.docstoc.com/docs/44501428/Report-on-the-Socio-Economic-Conditions-of-Muslims-in-India>, accessed 11 September 2011.

Ahmed Nassem (2001), *Liberation of Muslim women*, Delhi, Kalpaz Publication.

Basu, P. (2010), *Post Modernism, Marxism, Post-colonialism*. Kolkata, Avenel Press.

Bhargava, Rajeev, (2007), 'On the Persistent Political Under-Representation of Muslims in India', *Law and Ethics of Human Rights* (Vol. 1, Iss. 1).

Census of India, (2011), Office of the Registrar General, Tables: Profiles by Main Religions: Muslims, New Delhi.

De Haan, Arjan (2011), Rescuing exclusion from the poverty debate: group disparities and social transformation in India, *ISS Working Paper no. 517*, March 2011, http://repub.eur.nl/res/pub/22626/wp517.pdf, accessed 12 May, 2012.

Engineer, Asghar, Ali (1999), *The Quran, Women and Modern Society*. New Delhi, Sterling Publishers Private Limited.

Engineer, Asghar, Ali (2013), *Islam, Women and Gender Justice*, New Delhi, Gyan Publishing House.

Engineer, Asghar Ali (2007), *Muslim Women in Indian Society* <http://www.csss-isla.com/arch%2071.htm, accessed 9 September 2011.

Engineer, I. (2012), 'Political Leadership, Mobilisation and Violence', in A. Shaban, (ed.), *Lives of Muslims in India: Politics, Exclusion and Violence*, New Delhi, Routledge.

Hasan, Z. (2000), *Politics and the State in India*, New Delhi, Oxford University Press.

Hasan, Zoya and Menon, Ritu, (2004), *Unequal Citizens – A Study of Muslim Women in India*, New Delhi, Oxford University Press.

Hashemi, S. S. Schuler, and A. Riley. (1996), "Rural Credit Programs and Women's Empowerment in Bangladesh." *World Development*, 24(4).

Khalidi, O. (1995), *Indian Muslims Since Independence*, New Delhi, Vikas Publishing House.

Kirmani, N. (2009). Claiming Their Space: Muslim Women-led Networks and Women's Movement in India, *International Journal of Women's Studies*, Volume 9.

Menon, H. Z. (2004), *Unequal Citizens: A Study of Muslim Women in India*. New Delhi, Oxford University Press.

8

Muslim Women in the Context of Sachar Committee Report: Reference to Mayabunder Tehsil, North Andaman

Anita Banerjee

Introduction

Women have for ages been treated as unequal. No matter how modern a society develops, generally women are still treated as second class citizens the world over. Otherwise, how does one justify a basic right of humans to choose their representatives, the right to participate in the electoral process was given to them much after it had been conferred to their male counterparts? The first country to confer such rights was New Zealand, and that too in 1893. It is not just in the domain of public affairs but in every aspect of life we often hear the term, "the need to empower women". So it is quite self-evident that women need to be empowered, that they do not share equal rights in every domain of life. This discrimination is even more glaring when it comes to women belonging to the minority community. In fact, when we talk of minority it is not just related to people belonging to a particular religion caste or creed. Females as such belong to the class of minority, be it a Hindu, a Muslim or a Sikh or for that matter any other religion.

Position of Minority Women in the West

The western perception of minority women and their position in society is well reflected in Okin's book (Susan Moller Okin) "Is Multiculturalism bad for women?" She argues that only western societies provide equal rights to women whereas other minority religions, mainly non-Christians tend to subordinate females. Further "The Guardian" (7th Dec. 2012) reports that ethnic minority women are removing their *hijab* and making their names sound more English in order to combat discrimination and increase their chances of absorption in the job market. The report also states that in spite of their efforts the rate of joblessness among the ethnic minority women has refused to decline particularly in case of women from Bangladesh, Pakistan and other Black communities. Research by Professor Yoajun Li also found that it was very tough for Muslim Pakistani and Bangladeshi women to find work in the west as compared to women from other religions.

Position of Minority Women in India

India is one of the largest democracies in the world. It is also home to one of the largest minorities. Among the major religious groups Muslims dominate the minorities in India. The position of women in Islam has been a subject of various controversies even among the educated Muslims. This issue has further intensified under the influence of western liberalisation. The subject of Muslim women's rights has been a much debated subject. There is also general agreement that major problems of Muslim women are rooted in the Muslim society as a whole (Monica &Poonam, 2013). But a surprising and positive fact which has come to light through the present Census of 2011 is that the sex ratio of Muslims is better than that of the Hindus. It stands at 951 females per thousand males where as among Hindus it is 939 females. Even in terms of fertility, the decline in fertility is higher among Muslims than among the Hindus. The picture below shows the population of minorities in a descending order.

Table 8.1: Distribution of Population at National Level by Religion During Census, 2011

Religion	Number (Percent of the Population)
Hindu	**96.63 crore (79.8%)**
Muslim	**17.22 crore (14.2%)**
Christian	**2.78 crore (2.3%)**
Sikh	**2.08 crore (1.7%)**
Buddhist	**0.84 crore (0.7%)**
Jain	**0.45 crore (0.4%)**
Other Religion and Persuations (ORP)	**0.79 crore (0.7%)**
Religion not stated	**0.29 crore (0.2%)**

Population trends for major religious groups show that the growth rate of Muslim population is increasing but the pace of increase has declined over the period from 1951 to 2011. But in case of other religious groups the trend shows that after 2001 the population of all major religious groups has registered a decrease except that of the Muslim population below:

Objectives of the Present Study

1. To study the progress of Muslim women in terms of selected variables in Andaman and Nicobar Islands with special reference to Mayabunder Tehsil.
2. To study the level of awareness regarding the schemes related to the minority community (particularly women).
3. Provide suggestions for generating awareness.

Methodology

For the purpose of study both published data and primary data were used. Population of minority women is widely dispersed; hence a purposive sampling in eight Panchayats of Mayabunder Tehsil was covered. A total of 100 Households were selected.

Table 8.2: Distribution of India's Population by Religious Communities 1881-2011 According to Census Reports**

Religious community	1881	1891	1901	1911	1921	1931	1941	1951	1961	1971	1981	1991	2001	2011
Hindus	75.09	74.24	72.87	71.68	70.73	70.67	69.46	84.98	83.4	82.7	82.3	81.5	80.5	79.8
Muslims	19.97	20.41	21.88	22.39	23.23	23.49	24.28	9.91	10.7	11.2	11.8	12.12	13.43	14.23
Christians	0.71	0.77	0.98	1.21	1.47	1.77	1.91	2.35	2.4	2.6	2.4	2.3	2.3	2.3
Sikhs	0.74	0.68	0.77	1.00	1.06	1.28	1.46	1.74	1.8	1.9	1.9	1.9	1.9	1.72
Buddhists	0.07	0.09	0.10	0.11	0.12	0.13	0.12	0.05	0.7	0.7	0.7	0.8	0.8	0.70
Jains	0.49	0.51	0.47	0.41	0.39	0.37	0.37	0.45	0.5	0.5	0.5	0.4	0.4	0.37
Other Religions	2.92	3.30	2.92	3.21	3.01	2.30	2.41	0.53	0.3	0.4	0.4	0.4	0.6	0.89

** Indices for 1881-1941 apply to un-partitioned India and for 1951 to 2011 to the Republic of India.

Position of Women in Andaman Islands

The Islands of Andaman and Nicobar Groups has a total population of 3.81 lakhs. Position of women in Andaman and Nicobar Islands in general are better than in any other states. Though in terms of sex ratio it is lagging behind the national average 940 as against the islands sex ratio being 876. The distribution of population by religion in the islands is given below in Table 8.3. It is quite evident from the Table that Muslims constitute the second in terms of minority population (8.52%). The largest minority population being that of Christians, the Ministry of Minority Affairs, Government of India has identified Nicobar as a Minority Concentration District among the 90 total districts in the country. Studies on minority have been conducted in Nicobar district by Centre for Studies in Social Sciences, Calcutta under Minority Concentration District (MCD) project sponsored by ICSSR in 2006-07. The study focuses on one particular community that is the Christian community as Nicobar comprises mainly Christian population.

The islands of Andaman and Nicobar comprise three districts namely, South Andaman District, Nicobar District and North and Middle Andaman District. Nicobar Island has a concentration of Christian Minority. Muslims are to be found more in numbers in South Andaman.

Sachar Committee and Muslim Women

Sachar Committee was appointed with a view to preparing a report on the social, economic and educational status of Indian Muslims. However, the significant points to be noted in the context of Andaman and Nicobar Islands are that Muslims constitute only 8.52 percent of the total population and they are dispersed over the entire length and breadth of the island.

Discrimination as such of any kind does not exist in any form. Recommendations laid down by the Sachar Committee have not been followed in toto. The reason is obvious; there is lack of awareness among the minority population. Hence, the simple logic is – unless and until there is a build up of pressure things don't move at required speed. The committee has no women member in the panel, which itself is very unfortunate in a survey of social scenario among Muslims. Another unfortunate aspect regarding the committee is that it had suggested creating mass awareness as the first step towards the implementation of the report which has not been carried out as the findings of the survey below reveal.

Table 8.3: Distribution of Population by Religion in A&N Islands, Census, 2011

Religion	Population	Percentage (Percent)
Hindu	**2,64,296**	**69.45**
Christian	**80,984**	**21.28**
Muslim	**32,413**	**8.52**
Sikh	**1,286**	**0.34**
Not Available	**669**	**0.18**
Other Religion	**564**	**0.15**
Buddhist	**338**	**0.09**
Jain	**31**	**0.01**

Minorities in North and Middle Andaman

The district of North and Middle Andaman was created by bifurcating the erstwhile Andaman district in 2006. The district comprises three Tehsil which are Diglipur, Rangat, and Mayabunder. The district has a population of 105,539 as per the Census of 2011. It has a population density of 32 persons per sq. kilometer. It has a sex ratio of 925 females per 1000 males. For the purpose of study Mayabunder Tehsil was deliberately chosen. Information was collected from the female respondents using a structured questionnaire. There are total of eight Panchayats under Mayabunder Tehsil. Purposive samples of 100 respondents from total of eight Panchayats were collected.

The minority population of this District comprises mainly two kinds: The Moplahs (also called Mappilahs) are the Muslim community belonging to Malabar. Their ancestors came from Arab country in the Ninth century married local women and proselytised a very large number of natives (Census report 1881). The second groups of minority women are those who migrated from Uttar Pradesh through marriage. These Muslims have come to the islands for business purpose. The status of these women was assessed in terms of certain selected variables. A total of 100 women were surveyed in Mayabunder Tehsil. Since the population of minorities is widely dispersed, hence the number of women selected from each of the Panchayats was not uniform. Approximately six to seven of women were purposively selected for the purpose of survey. Broadly, three variables were chosen to judge the status of women. Wearing of *Burkha or Hijab* is a symbol of their tradition; however, in the islands there doesn't seem to be a compulsion in terms of attire of women in general. A break up of women as per their qualification reveals during the survey that majority of women, 63 percent in this category whose qualification is below Xth standard, wear either *Hijab* (A scarf that covers the head and neck but leaves the face clear) or a *Burka* (covers the entire face and body) out of personal choice where as 32 percent wears it due to some kind of compulsion, this category includes women who hail from "Maullana family". In fact, women in general wear *burqa or hijab* ("Mafta" commonly used term for *hijab*) because they want to follow the customs and want to keep the tradition alive (this is true of women irrespective of their academic qualification). Those women who are a bit higher in the educational ladder (having educational qualification above class XII std.) and are exposed to Mainland culture wear a *hijab or burqa* occasionally (74%). This trend is prevalent among all categories of women though the percentage varies. There is another tendency observed among the women which can be attributed to what is termed as "demonstration effect" (imitating of consumption habits). It was observed during the survey that the practice of wearing *burqa* in particular was prevalent among migrants from Uttar Pradesh who had migrated through marriage. In fact the freedom to exercise their personal choice is almost directly proportional to their academic qualification.

Table 8.4: Status of Women in Mayabunder Tehsil by Educational Qualification

Educational Qualification	Wearing of *Burkha/Hijab*		
	Compulsion	Personal Choice	Demonstration Effect
Below Xth	32	63	5
X to XII	20	72	8
Above XII	12	74	14

Another interesting fact which came to light during the survey was that majority of women have not even heard of Sachar Committee which has been constituted for the upliftment of women of this community (89%, 86% and 70% of women of all three categories) are totally in the dark about this Committee. Only seven percent of those having educational qualification above XII have reported that they are aware of such Committee because of which OBC status was granted to pre-1942 settlers.

The third variable which was used to assess the position of women was their decision-making power. Here again only 67 percent of women (who were a little higher in the educational status) categorically asserted that they had the liberty to take decisions at home and that their decision was considered very crucial for the family. Whereas 44 percent among those who had not passed even Xth class and 36 percent of those with qualification between Xth and XII were ambiguous in their response to the question of freedom in decision-making, sometimes they had been and sometimes not even consulted.

Table 8.5: Status of Women in Mayabunder Tehsil Knowledge about Sachar Committee by Educational Qualification

Educational Qualification	Knowledge about Sachar Committee		
	Not heard	Just heard	Aware
Below X	89	9	2
X to XII	86	11	3
Above XII	70	23	7

Table 8.6: Status of Women in Mayabunder Tehsil Having Decision Making Power by Educational Qualification

Educational Qualification	Decision Making Power		
	Does Not have	Sometimes	Has the power
Below Xth	12	32	56
X to XII	07	29	64
Above XII	06	27	67

Table 8.7: Details of Voting Pattern among Different Groups of Minority Women in Mayabunder Tehsil

According to origin of minority	Party basis	Husband's choice	Women centric issues
Mophlas	58	35	7
Migrants from U.P	62	29	9
Others	61	33	6

In order to determine minority women's freedom in the matter of governance, a survey regarding their voting pattern was also conducted. The findings revealed that in the matter of casting their valuable votes all (those who were covered under the survey) women preferred to cast vote on the basis of Political Party, irrespective of whether they were Moplahs or migrants from Uttar Pradesh or other Muslim women (Bengali Muslim, Tamil etc.). Around 35 percent of Moplah women and 29 percent of Migrants from UP voted in favour of their husbands' choice. Women centric issues were not found to be a predominant factor while casting their vote as is evident from the Table 8.7.

Conclusion

The study reveals that the status of minority women in the islands is not so much related to the external factors, meaning thereby to the discrimination outside their homes on account of their belonging to a particular community. In fact, the findings suggest that they are just like other women (women from other communities) in terms of their position in the society. With more and more women taking to education there is a gradual change in this group of women. However, a very disheartening fact which has come to light is that there is all but a total ignorance regarding the committee and its recommendations. So, as suggested by the committee the first step required in this direction is creation of more and more awareness.

REFERENCES

Chandramouli, C. (2013), *Census of India 2001, Primary Census Abstract, Total Population.* Table 1-A Indian Series-1, New Delhi, Office of the Registrar General and Census Commissioner.

Minority Concentration District Project, Nicobar, A&N islands, sponsored by Ministry of Minority Affairs. Govt. of India.

Minority Report (Muslim for Secular Democracy (MSD).

Monica Munjial & Poonam Kaushik, (2013), "Muslim Women and Minority Rights in India", *Mainstream*, Vol. LI, No. 12.

Press Information Bureau, Govt., of India, Ministry of Minority Affairs, 21 Feb., 2014.

Susan Moller Okinn (2000), "Is Multiculturism Bad for Women?", in *The Times Higher Education.*

https://censusindia.gov.in/census.website/data/census-table.

Part-Three
Socio-Cultural Diversity and Islands Muslims

9

Marriage, Society and Cultural Diversity among Island's Muslims

Hema Bannerjee

Introduction

Indian Muslims constitute around 15 percent of the country's population. In all respects they play an important role in the socio-economic and cultural scenario of Indian society. However, a sizeable section of them are found to be socially, politically and economically backward (Sachar, 2006). The outcome of the Sachar Committee report has opened the eyes of Indian Governance and society regarding the plight of our second largest community in India after 60 years of Independence. Even after six decades of our democratic governance, we could not streamline our largest religious minority in the track of welfare and development. They are still used as vote banks for political gains by political parties without bothering about their real welfare and progress.

Illiteracy, ignorance and poverty are some of the main reasons responsible for their backwardness and has resulted in a small section of youth engaging in anti-national activities.They experience day to day discrimination in education, employment, housing and public services which has created discontentment in the minds of poor Muslims who feel alienated from the mainstream of Indian society.

The State of Origin of Indian Muslims

The Majority of the Indian Muslims state of origin is India. A good number of them are descendents of Indian Hindus. In the North, the immigration of Islam happened as rulers, whereas, in South, they came as traders (Irfan, 2012). The settlement of Muslims in Kerala along the coastal areas of Malabar and Travancore happened in the Seventh Century. Since their arrival, a socio-cultural synthesis with the local Hindus has developed and these small groups have gradually accepted the Indian way of life, customs and manners in their lives. According to Amartya Sen, the poor Muslims were descendents of lower caste Hindus who had converted to Islam (sometimes to escape caste-based discrimination). (Sen and Jeans, 2013). Ms. Zarina Bhatty opined that almost all Muslims are converts from Hinduism, they accepted Islam as interpreted by the *mullaha* ...... The new religion did not change their everyday life much (Ziya Us Salam, 2016). Hence, many Muslim rulers were descendents of Hindus. The Islamic culture in South India has revealed that in many cases in life cycles, the Muslims followed Hindu rituals centring round birth, marriage and death, retention of Hindu manners. Therefore, Davis, a historian said

> "The spread of Islam has been a gradual process .... to win over the support of local people either by converting them or by pacifying them. Therefore, Muslims partly because of socio-cultural compulsion and partly because of strategy, adopted local rituals and practices while allowing the converts to retain most of their habits and customs. It is not surprising that many of the nominal converts retained much of the former religion and indeed Islam underwent considerable Hindustanisation in India". (Chand, 1946)

Cultural assimilation is so strong in Indian society. This is the foundation of Indian Secular aspect. According to Abdul Shaban and

Abusaleh Sharief "the religious assimilations is so conscious across India that it is easy to mix it altogether ……The Sufi saints of the subcontinent are revered both by Muslims and Hindus. Assimilation is so strong that Hindu parents let *imams* at local mosque serve as a traditional healers for their children, with *dua* or Islamic prayer. In many parts in India, Muslim marriages are solemnised by the groom tying an amulets to his bride that is known as a *tali* among Hindus" (Shaban and Sharief, 2016).

Early Andaman Society

Islands society is the admixture of all religions /communities who live peacefully with national integrity. Andaman society developed with the origin of Penal Settlement of Indian convicted prisoners in 1858. This society has become a symbol of progress with social harmony and dignity for all minorities including six indigenous tribals. Muslims constitute nine percent of the islands population, contributing in business and other social sectors along with other communities. In this vibrant society, the Muslims are cordial, liberal and progressive. The females are highly respected. To build a new society in the pre-independent India, British needed equal ratio of both sexes in the newly built Penal Colony in Andaman. However, they faced the paucity of female members in Penal society.

Table 9.1: Distribution of Male-Female Ratio in Convicted Society during 1874-1901

Year	Male	Percentage	Female	Percentage	Total
1874	6733	95.25	336	4.75	7069 (100%)
1881	10325	90.16	1127	9.84	11452 (100%)
1891	10874	92.64	864	7.36	11738 (100%)
1901	11217	93.89	730	6.11	11947(100%)

In the first batch 159 female convicts who were brought from mainland, 117 were Hindus and 42 were Muslims of which 10 were below 20 years, 72 were in between 20 and 30 years and 43 in the age group of 30-40 years and the remaining 34 were above 40 years. However, out of 159, 134 were widows and 25 married.

The male-female ratio in Penal Society was 10:1. The issue of shortage of women had a serious impact on the social history of Andaman society and especially on women's position. As Aparna Vaidik rightly said,

> "the official machinery often invoked the scarcity of female to justify the local crime rate and the prevalence of prostitution or homosexuality in the colonies ...... held it up as a reason for the exploitation of female population. It was felt that the competition over limited sexual resources created jealousies and rivalries, which led to instances of crime and subjected women to exploitation by male labourers and *sirdars* and led to polyandry and extra marital relations". (Vaidik, 2006).

To overcome this serious issue, the Penal authority had offered the wives of male convicts in Andaman to join their husbands and start a new life. The jail authorities in Alipore and other jails in India were asked to send female convicts in Andaman. The main objective of this policy was to fill the gap and to improve male and female ratio and thus to bring about a control over sexual crimes and homosexuality in Andaman society. But the policy could not succeed because the Hindu females feared that they would lose their orthodox Hindu identity/caste, so they were reluctant to embark the ship and join their husbands in Andaman. Only few convicted females who were being convicted for murdering husband or infants -which were being considered the most heinous crimes accepted the offer.

Hence, scarcity of females or eligible bride in Andaman Penal society compelled the male convicts especially Hindus to marry girls of other religions (Muslim) and to change their religion.In many cases Hindu orthodox parents disowned their sons forcing them to live in their-in-law's house by converting themselves to

Table 9.2: Decadal Variation of Religion-wise Population in A and N Islands during1901-2011

Religion	1901	1931	1941	1951	1961	1971	1981	1991	2001	2011
Hindu	9264 (37.5)	7618 (25.8)	8427 (24.9)	9294 (30.00)	32781 (51.58)	70143 (60.91)	121793 (64.52)	189521 (67.52)	264589 (69.23)	264313 (69.45)
Muslim	4201 (17.1)	6719 (22.8)	8005 (23.71)	4783 (15.44)	7398 (11.64)	11655 (10.12)	16188 (8.57)	21354 (7.60)	29265 (8.22)	32425 (8.25)
Christian	486 (1.97)	1461 (4.95)	2613 (7.73)	9494 (30.65)	17973 (28.28)	30342 (26.35)	48274 (25.57)	67211 (23.94)	77178 (21.66)	80581 (21.28)
Animist	8399 (34.07)	9955 (33.38)	11076 (32.80)	NA	NA	NA	NA	NA	NA	NA
Others	2299	3710	3647	7400	5396	3002	2486	2575	3100	2930
Total	**24649 (100.00)**	**29463 (100.00)**	**33768 (100.00)**	**30971 (100.00)**	**63548 (100.00)**	**115133 (100.00)**	**188741 (100.00)**	**280661 (100.00)**	**356152 (100.00)**	**380581 (100.00)**

*Animist are including Tribals of A&N Islands.

wife's religion. Hence, Prof. Vaidik rightly said that most of the Muslims families have had a history of being disowned by the community of the Hindu parents on his /her marriage with a Muslim. (Vaidik, 2006).

In 1951 Census the Nicobari tribals were included under Christianity. The population in Penal settlement had increased with the arrival of Moplahs from Kerala, Bhantus from Central India and Karen from Burma after 1922. The sudden increase in individuals affected the settlement life in terms of the diversity of population and also religious compositions in Local society (Dhingra, 2005). The religious statistics between 20s and 30s has shown increase in the Muslim population due to arrival of 1,885 Moplahs and decline in Hindu population. Immediately after independence, the rehabilitation schemes of Government of India had started and more than three thousand Bengali Hindu refugee families from East Pakistan were settled in Andaman Islands. As a result, the Hindu population showed an increase from 9,294 in 1951 to 32,781 in 1961. However, the Hindu-Muslim population ratio in 1941 was almost equal i.e. Muslims 8005 (23.71%) and Hindus 8,427 (24.9%). Indeed the post-independent scenario of Muslim population is that their population has been declining subsequently as per Census from 1961 to 2011compared to population of both Hindus and Christians in the same period. The increase in Hindu population has been mainly because of the settlement of Bengali families in rural Andaman which is 23 percent-24 percent of total population in the Islands on an average as shown in every Census since 1951 onwards.

Marital Relations Among Andaman Society

The Andaman society allows inter-religion, inter-caste and inter-sect marriages. Hundreds of Moplahs who were transported between 1922-27 in Andaman from Madras jail were from Malabar province of Undivided Kerala. Moplahs preferred marriage with sub-sects i.e. Sunnis and Wahabis. However, Mrs. Kiran Dhingra has rightly pointed out that the Burmese turned increasingly for marriage partners to the Telugus, Tamils and Tribals communities, but Bhantus found affinities with the Bengalees ; the Karen with the Ranchis and Burmese and Moplahs found spouse within Bengali, Madrasi and Hindi speaking (Dhingra, 2005). Due to inter-religion and inter-community marriages, the descendents of Penal settlement were looked down upon by Indian officials because socially they did not strictly adhere to the orthodox customs of caste-religion; especially in matrimonial alliances (Majumder, 1975).

On the basis of time periods, the arrival of Muslims in Andaman and Nicobar can be divided into many categories. In the Penal Colonial phase (1858-1920), arrivals were convicted prisoners of 1857 Sepoy Mutiny and life-imprisonment criminals who were transported to *Kalapani* for capital punishment. Second phase (1921-27) witnessed the transportation of Moplahs of Malabar and Trivancore of Kerala from Madras jail. Altogether 1885 Moplahs out of which 714 of them were females were transported to Andaman. During these two phases Muslims remained in Andamans as free men and many Moplah males brought their families. Later they were categorised as "Local Born" along with the Indians who were transported before independence of India.

Third phase of arrival of Muslims started during Post-independence to engage themselves in Government jobs and also private activities. They were mostly from Kerala, Tamil Nadu, Uttar Pradesh, Gujarat, Bihar and West Bengal. After 90s a good number of Bengali Muslims have come as labourers, females as domestic help, petty business (hawker, Puchkawala, Vegetable and fruits vendors etc.) in city areas. Most of them were from 24 Parganas (South and North), Nadia, Medinipur, Maldah and Murshidabad districts of West Bengal.

The fourth category of Muslims are considered as those who were converted to Islam from Christianity among Nicobari tribals. In early twentieth century, the British allowed M/s Akhoojee Jedwet & Co. a Gujarati Muslim trader to start business in Car Nicobar island. His company brought labourers and officials from Gujarat to run the establishment in Nicobar district. As these staff stayed for a long time away from their homes, these young Muslim males started entering into marital relations with native girls. Most of these eligible bachelors or even married males who left their families in Gujarat started maintaining a family in Nicobar district.

> "Of late the number of Nicobari Muslims has increased in Car Nicobar and Nancowry islands with the advent of R Akoojee Jadwet during the British period. At that time some Nicobari certainly showed interest in embracing Islam partly because they were eager to adopt outside cultural traits including food habits and partly because they were spiritually enlightened and had access to certain privileges. Later, they also encouraged others to become Muslims" (Justine, 1990).

There is a strong evidence that for a long time, the foreign nationals from Malaysia, Indonesia who arrived at these tiny isolated islands like Pilo-Milo, Kundul, Dering, Trinket in Nancowry group of islands were welcomed by local Nicobari families without the notice of local authority. Their frequent arrivals resulted in establishing intimate relations with local families as well as religious conversions. As Nicobaris were simple and liberal, they did not mind their daughters marrying non-Christians and converting to Islam.

Secularism and Cultural Diversity

Education enlightens the society and empowers the individuals. Illiteracy breeds social evils, discrimination and inequality. Education is the vehicle of progress and freedom of individuals. The proper education is required for community progress and developments. Islands Muslims and other minorities are taking up education based on secular philosophy along with other communities. They are being absorbed in every sector of employment, business and profession. Females are more progressive and educated than their counterparts in other states in India. Education and multi-dimensional socio-cultural approach of local people has helped to make a unique society with a strong secular outlook.Inter-religion and inter-sect marriage is an old phenomenon in local society.

All festivals are equally celebrated by people of both religion. It was rightly observed by both Rizvi and Khan "a divorced Hindu women married a Muslim and then she got children from her Muslim husband. The children from her previous Hindu husband is visiting temple with the mother and the children from her Muslim husband visit Mosque and observe Muslim rituals". (Rizvi and Khan, 2014). Therefore, Prof. Aparna Vaidik has observed and concluded that "both Khairun Madam's son and Riyazuddin were uncomfortable regarding the non-Islamic character of one of the parents (Vaidik, 2006). It may be the personal feeling of Mrs. Khairun Madam's son and Riyazuddin, but as a whole, the Islamic society in Andaman is not isolatedly thinking about their dual religion identity, as because most of the Muslim family have had a history of being disowned by the community of the Hindu parents on his/her marriage with a Muslim.

Muslim society in Andaman is divisionless and classless. But in case of marriage and family relations, they follow sects and sub-sects as is followed in mainland India. All the families of Pre-independent India, irrespective of castes and religions, are receiving OBC reservation facilities in Government jobs and special quota in higher educational institutions in Mainland in professional courses. Though the population of Muslims in Andaman as per 2011 Census is 8.25 percent but their presence in Government jobs has more than doubled and is higher than all India average.

Conclusion

The former Vice President of India, Shri Hamid Ansari, the scholar and diplomat of contemporary India nicely illustrated the present day scenario of Indian Muslims which he delivered in his inaugural speech on the occasion of All India Majlis-e-Mushawarat Golden Jubilee in New Delhi on 31 August 2015. He quoted from The Quran and said "Verily (truly) never will God change it the condition of a people until they change it themselves with their own souls" (The Quran, S XII ii.). He further said that the leading educated Muslims .....should go beyond looking at questions of identity and dignity in a defensive mode and explore how both can be furthered in a changing Indian and a changing world. It should widen its ambit to hitherto unexplored or adequately explored requirement of all segments of the community particularly women, youth and non-elite section who together constitute the overwhelming majority (Ansari, 2015).

We can change our fate and future, if we work hard without blaming others. Mainstream education is the necessity of the day and religious fanatism has no place in a progressive society. Andaman model is a right and perfect model to understand true secularism and unity in diversity.

REFERENCES

Abdul Shaban and Abusaleh Sharief (2016), "No Country for Islamophobia", in *Indian Express*, 15.3.2016.

Ansari, Hamid, M. (2015), Inaugural Speech on Challenges before Indian Muslims Community in All India Majlis-e-Mushawarat Golden Jubilee, in *EPW*, Vol. L (40).

Biswas, Swapan K (2015), Religious conversion among Bay Islands Tribes. in *EPW*, (web exclusive).

Chandramouli, C (2013), *Census of India 2001, Primary Census Abstract, Total Population. Table 1-A India Series-1*, Office of the Registrar General and Census Commissioner, India, New Delhi.

Dhingra, Kiran (2005), "*The Andaman and Nicobar Islands, in the 20th Century, a Gazetter",* New Delhi, Oxford University Press.

Irfan, Mohammed (2012), *Social Exclusion Ethnography*, Jaipur, Aavishkar Publishers.

Justine. Austice (1990), *The Nicobarese* (ed) K S Singh, Calcutta, Seagull Books.

Majumder, R C (1975), *Penal Settlement in Andaman,* Ministry of Culture, Government of India.

Sachar, Rajendra. (2006), High Level Committee Report on Socio-economic and Educational Status of Muslim Community in India, Government of India, New Delhi.

Rizvi, S.H.N. and Iar Ali Khan (2014), *The Locals of Port Blair.* Delhi, B.R. Publishing Corporation.

Sen, Amartya and Jean Dreze (2014), *An Uncertain Glory; India and its contradictions*, Allen lane, UK, Penguin Books.

Tara Chand, (1946), *Influence of Islam and Indian Culture*, Allahabad, The Indian Press.

Vaidik, Aparna (2006), Settling the convicts; Matrimony and Domesticity in the Andamans. *Studies in History* 22(2), 2006, New Delhi, Sage Publications.

Zarina Bhatty (2016) Womam's right to divorce in Contested Practice by Ziya Us Salam in *Frontline*, June 24, 2016.

https://censusindia.gov.in/census.website/data/census-table.

10

Making of Tradition: Perspectives on Hindu–Muslim Relations in A and N Islands

Kanwar Chanderdeep Singh

Introduction and Problematisation

The making of traditions is often a conscious or a non-conscious exercise wherein the centripetal forces of history, culture, shared sorrows and happiness, longings and belongings play constructive roles. Many a time the made traditions blunt the divide of origin of the otherwise varied communities distinct from each other by ethnicity, language, religion and may be in some other aspects. The society and culture of a particular space and time often reflects the mooring of the people who live in those times and spaces. It is particularly apt for that group of people and places which/who do not have a very long history to remember and cherish. The place called Andaman and Nicobar Islands presents such a picture and give such an impression. This essay therefore tries to explore the inter-communal relations involving the Hindu and the Muslims of Andaman and Nicobar Islands and what factored these communities to live in amity in spite of marked communal conflagrations in different parts of India. I also intend to present an overview of the geo cum socio-cultural environs of these Islands which strategically are the one of the most important and sensitive regions of India.

There are simple but curious questions that arise out of dabbling with the concept of, 'invented traditions' in Andaman and Nicobar Islands. Why there is a need to study these invented traditions? More so, why should a history scholar study it at all? Why not any Social Anthropologist? The pertinence of these problems draws a historical inquiry into it. The invented traditions of any society in any spatial time frame are indicative of different socio-psychological undercurrents. The problem of intangibility as well as unavailability of the sources to construct past can therefore be eased by the study of such invented practices. There may be reasons to the differential functionality of the traditions. The Andaman traditions also need to be studied to get a fair idea of people's past who migrated or brought to this place even at the cost of severing cultural and kinship ties. Here arises the role of a historian who dugs into the historical legitimacy of newly invented traditions at a newer place doing juxtapositional exercises vis-à-vis the past and present. To invoke Hobsbawm who decodes thus about the three some invented traditions-(a) those establishing or symbolising social cohesion or membership of groups, real or artificial communities, (b) those establishing the legitimacy of institutions, status or relations of authority and (c) those whose main purpose was socialisation, inculcation of beliefs, value systems and conventions of behaviour (Eric, 1995). These aspects in varying degrees can be seen in the socio-cultural milieu of Island society.

As far as the Andaman Nicobar Islands is concerned nothing substantial has been said about the phenomenon of invented traditions and hence an appropriate social discourse has not been set or at least adequately investigated. This place though has many communal and ethnic groups and problematisation of all may not fit to the size of a limited length academic paper. Hence I shall focus majorly on two of the three biggest communities of these Islands; the Hindus and Muslims and their made (invented) traditions. What are the socio-cultural traditions that have bonded the people together despite the overwhelming religious markers scattered all around the Islands particularly in the capital city of Port Blair? Particularly, these markers elsewhere in India have a chequered record of contributing to religious antagonisms.

Communally diverse and charged country as India has become since the beginning of twentieth century, the inter-faith relations have always been an issue of intense debates and contestations. The two most important communities or religions of this nation that are more often in the centre stage of discourse on communal harmony and acrimony are the Hindus and Muslims. Not long before, the *Shuddhi* versus *Tabligh* and *Sangathan* versus *Tanzeem* like movements created conducive atmosphere for communal polarisations in British India and pitted the Hindus and Muslims against each other. The socio-religious reform movements of late nineteenth and early twentieth centuries hence were one of the biggest contributors towards the deterioration of inter-communal relations in pre-independence India, other being the British. The British benefited from pitting Hindus and Muslims against one another and portrayed themselves as neutral saviours who could keep ancient religious conflicts at bay (Truschke, 2015). When bad politics fed on radicalisation, the resultant effect was the partition of India on communal lines. It is also believed that most of communal conflicts in modern India have either fuelled by the ideological assumptions, mythical or historical and by the politics of mollification. Various politico-religious issues like the cow-protection, uniform civil code and proselytisation have furthered the antagonising tendencies between them. The pre-independence Jinnah-nian notion of Hindus and Muslims being separate nations therefore still echoes in some sections of the people and the ideal of secularism is still struggling to find its true definition in Indian context.

A noted writer and journalist Francois Gautier with a keen eye on the Indian socio-politics observed,

On the surface, you cannot find two more dissimilar religions: the first one is a monotheistic faith which proclaims that Allah is the only God and all believers of other religions are to be treated as “Infidels”; and the second swears by polytheism and adores thirty millions of Gods and Goddesses… Because of these differences, both these creeds have been at loggerhead for centuries and the Muslim invasions of India have been exceptionally bloody. Today even, Islam and Hinduism collide in Kashmir, in Ayodhya, or in the wars between Pakistan and India (Imperial Gazetteer, 1994).

Having said that, majority of these two majority communities who have a long shared history of more than 1200 years wherefore via processes of acculturation have brought in them a sense of mutual agreement and acceptance.

Hindus-Muslims Syncretism and Cosmopolitanism of Andamans

Andaman and Nicobar Islands' tryst with modernity began with the settlement at Chatham Island in 1787 when the British Government of Bengal set up her naval base. However, it was abandoned shortly due to the hostile living conditions predominantly due to malaria. In the wake of the rebellion of 1857, the British again decided to resettle these Islands with the convicts on more durable and permanent basis in 1858. The high point of the colonial tradition of crime and punishment culminated in the form of the construction of the Cellular Jail in 1906 (started in 1896). The process of influx of outsiders that started off with the penalising intent did not stop with the end of colonial rule. In the decolonised India it continued unabated though the nature and character of immigration changed and so were its dimensions. In the wake of pre-1942 and post-1947 migrations to these Islands its demographical profile underwent a monumental change with the sons of the soil (tribal) becoming minority. Through various policy measures the Government populated these islands with the people from pan India. Predominantly, the states of West Bengal, Andhra Pradesh, Tamil Nadu, Kerala, Chotta Nagpur region of Jharkhand and to some extent Punjab became the major contributors towards this cause of 'Indianisation' of these Islands. In the present times, at best, we can describe the social fabric of Andaman Nicobar Islands as cosmopolitan.

The communities which came to these Islands pre- and post-Independence brought with them the slices of their culture and heritage and thus laid the foundation of a new synthetic culture. This culture was the healthy concoction of the several pan-Indian traditions which hitherto had not tasted each other. So the phenomenon of the formation of the Andamanese society is not of a distant past and was a process primarily and loosely started after the colonisation. The evolution of Andaman Nicobar Islands first as penal colony and later on as a Union Territory presents a picture of cultural universalism and relative similitude. In spite of the seemingly different communities that inhabit these Islands, they mostly converge on varied aspects on social and communal life. Along with carrying the baggage of their past native places they have successfully metamorphosed themselves in accordance with norms of a cosmopolitan society. An unintended legacy of colonial rule, both British and a small Japanese interlude (1942-45) was the cultural and communal harmonisation. The acculturative phenomenon mentioned in the preceding paragraphs therefore seems more pronounced in these Islands than anywhere else in the country. There are varied plausible factors to this blending of traditions.

According to the Census of 2011 the number of Hindus and Muslims in Andaman Nicobar Islands are 264296 and 32413 respectively which makes them around 69.45 percent and 8.52 percent of the total population. Although the Hindus and the Muslims are among the biggest communities but they are seldom homogeneous. Both communities could trace their antecedents to diverse geo-cultural regions of the Indian subcontinent. Saving the tribal, the ex-convicts of different religious dispensations and their descendents (Local Borns) are the earliest settlers of these Islands. The Hindus and Muslims were brought from all parts of India as convicts as well as free settlers. However, at several specific junctures in the history of these islands the influx of Hindus and Muslims was the greatest. First instance came in the aftermath of Moplah rebellion in the Malabar region from 1921 to 1923 when large numbers of Muslim Moplah convicts were incarcerated to Andaman and lead to a big surge in the Muslim population. The second important surge was led by the deportation of the members of Bhantu community, mainly Hindus purportedly of Kshatriya lineage. The third upsurge came immediately after the Partition of India when the displaced Bengalis from East Pakistan were rehabilitated in the Islands in 1949 followed by a Five Year Colonisation plan begun in 1952 (Sinha, 1952). The migrations to the Islands in the wake of Partition of India particularly from East Pakistan alarmed the local people and generated a sense of insecurity of being marginalised by becoming minority. It affected the communal harmony and increased racial tensions. The next influx though somewhat illegal came in the wake of the formation of Bangladesh in 1971-72 and many Muslims apart from the Hindus managed to get permanent shelter here. In addition to the above mentioned various settlers from South India like Travancore-Cochin and Madras state have contributed towards the demographic fulfilment of Andaman Nicobar Islands.

Examples of Hybridisation

The hybridisation of society with strong inter-faith linkages can be vividly seen in the common life of the populace. The examples are galore which represent such hybridisation. Broadly speaking, such intermingling could be understood by looking at four different facets of social life *viz.* matrimony, culinary and dietary habits, language and festival celebration.

Marriage is such a social institution in India where the norms are strongly guided by the communal and caste customary practices. Any digression from the established normative behavioural codes expectedly generates strong reactions. A country where honour killings are still rampant and are accepted as a way of redeeming family and community pride among the sections of society in the mainland India, Andaman and Nicobar Islands (ANI) presents a stark non-conformist picture. The extent to which interfaith marriage is possible and the degree of social and religious institutions' acceptance of interfaith couples indicate the breadth and depth of social pragmatism. The tradition of inter-marriages goes back to 1870s when the contact between free settlers continued and self supporters expanded. The number of marriages in the penal settlement rose sharply as a result from 69 in 1876-77 to 109 in 1877-78. Inter-marriages between free settlers and self-supporters were fundamentally inconsistent with policies of segregation but given the centrality of marriage to rehabilitation scheme in Andamans, the regime willingly compromised on segregation (Sen, 2000). There was shortage of women before and after independence which proved like blessing in a way. Since the women were few and therefore the men had very little choice. There were the instances of Hindus marrying Buddhists, Buddhists marrying Muslims, Muslims marrying Sikhs (Singh, 1978). The trend initiated because of the exigencies of penalty and survivals continued in the twentieth century and well post 1947.

Even in the far flung tribal Nicobar group of Islands the inter-faith matrimony is quite rampant among the tribal, either Christian or Muslim or a Hindu animist. The conversions based on these marriages are taken in stride without any associated outrage or ill will against the other, a phenomenon common in mainland India. It has been observed in a study regarding the socio-cultural aspects of the locals where a divorced Hindu woman married a Muslim and then got children from her Muslim husband. The children from her previous Hindu husband were visiting temple with the mother and the children from her Muslim husband were visiting mosque and observed Muslim rituals, no confrontation was ever reported (Khan and Rizvi, 2014). In a same family we may have a Hindu husband, a Muslim wife and Christian cousins. Andaman experience thus shows that marrying someone of another faith tends to improve one's view of that faith bringing about harmonisation based on heterogeneity.

The food in these Islands is a great conglomerateur. Generally it is believed that the Hindus tend to lean more towards vegetarianism whereas the Muslims are ubiquitously non-vegetarians. However, the geography, restricted availability of vegetables as well as heavy cross–cultural interactions has altered the dietary habits of the locals of all faiths. When compared to the mainland more percentage of

Hindus have adopted non-vegetarian dietary habits. Even *Biryanis* in these Islands do not distinguish between the Hindus or the Muslims or for that matter the Christians. Ubiquitous consumption of the *halal* non vegetarian food (ungrudgingly even by the Hindus) is another point of cultural synthesis and accommodation. All the prominent Indian festivals are celebrated with equal camaraderie irrespective of their being belonging to the other side of communal spectrum. While my fieldwork I came across two peculiar spectacles of *Ganesha Visarjan* and *Durga Visarjan* wherein the jubilant crowd accompanying these twin processions were curiously inter-communal. Dancing to the film tunes they scrupulously merged their identities to a common whole bothering the least about the segregative popular understanding of their religions. The point I wish to make is that the similar occasions at several places in mainland I had historically been the harbinger communal riots between the Hindus and Muslims (Brass, 2003). The Andaman Nicobar Islands is diametrically antithetical in this context.

The mother tongues of the local population are as numerous as in the parts of India from where it is derived. At the time in 1950s and 1960s when India was being re-organised on linguistic basis and lingual rivalries were running large within the states, Andaman and Nicobar Islands emerged as a perfect prototype of a nationalism based upon language. According to the Imperial Gazetteer of India Provincial Series, Andaman and Nicobar Islands, the *lingua franca* of the Settlement was Urdu (Hindustani), spoken in very possible variety of corruption and with every variety of accents. It is also the vernacular of the 'local born' whatever their descent was (Imperial Gazetter, 1994). Presently, Andaman Creole Hindi is the *lingua franca* in Islands and has successfully managed to cement the communal ties. It draws its vocabulary from linguistic traditions of all the communities inhabiting the Islands. In spite of great diversity in languages the unity prevails in expression which is largely facilitated by Hindustani, a fusion of linguistic pragmatism with Andamanese identity. Hence the lingual tradition has effectively managed to contain the 'us versus them' conflict which otherwise could have marred the communal solidarity as Hindi versus Urdu and Hindi versus Punjabi controversy has done in the cases of Uttar Pradesh and Punjab.

Historical Antecedents

In question is the Hindu-Muslim relationship. The imperatives that have made Hinduism and Islam to thrive together could be found in the one and half century history of the societal construct of the Islands. These communities have passed through three different phases of domination and authority which has aided in the formulation of their invented traditions. The first cycle was under the British rule with its crime and punishment tautology, people getting used to it and accepting it as a tradition. The second phase constituting Japanese regime, with the tradition of no crime but suspicion, resultant punishment and people getting abused due to that. The third phase was and is under the Indian governance with its bureaucratic stranglehold and intricacies, a natural corollary of the modern democratic set-up with an overflowing idea of nationalism. Here again the people imbibing the idea, reworked their relation with the authority and institutions and in the process making themselves a part of it. There are another set of traditions which are obvious outcomes of togetherness; geographic and historic.

In the Island society social and cultural innovations are quite a recent phenomenon whose concretisation roughly started after reduction in penalising intent of the colonialists. These invented traditions are ostensibly relevant even today because of the presence of the element of contemporaneity in them. The language, the communal relations, demography and the shared baggage of history that people carry feed on these traditions. Had ANI been a separate state, its unity would have been a match for the Singaporean nation state, a colonial cousin which providentially had the tryst with nationalism broadly at the same time. The communal binaries of Hindu-Muslim could even had been lesser concretised. However, that would have been again a constructed tradition which could have come to them naturally. The conjecture in this regard could be drawn *vis à vis* mainland India where both the antique traditions of *Bharatvarsha* as well as the concocted ones of 'Hindu Rashtra' were galvanising the anti-colonial struggle and the phenomenon of nation in making. Understandably, traditions, invented or original ones were templates on which the claims and counter-claims straddle.

The people of Andaman and Nicobar Islands have seen the dark days of penalisation under the British and even darker under the Japanese regime. This had a solidifying effect on the fraternal bondage of the people of diverse origins. If taken into account the early period of settlement of the Islands it is found that Port Blair (which had single largest concentration of the population) failed to develop a genuinely collaborationist class of natives. As Satadru Sen argues that the convict subordination retained a persistent sense of solidarity with other convicts and their failure to function as reliable agents of state surveillance reflects an agenda of politically united opposition to the colonial regime (Sen, 2000). This depicts that even in the initial stages of settlement in the Islands a sense of unity had started prevailing even though the aftermath of the 1857 generated much acrimony among the Hindus and the Muslims who blamed each other of sabotaging the spirit of revolt. There are two instances depicted here among many such instances where the initial Hindu-Muslim repulsiveness was explicitly discernible. As back as in 1859 writing to the Home Department, Superintendent Haughton noted the difficulty in getting Hindu convicts to eat food cooked at the Settlement hospital where the Muslim sick were treated (Haughton, 1859). Secondly, in the last quarter of nineteenth century many Wahabis were transported to ANI which helped the cause of Islamic radicalisation of the Islands. In Port Blair, as elsewhere, a great resort for those desiring to raise their social status was the adoption of Islam (Singh, 1978). One such Wahabi was Mohd. Jaffar Thaneshwari, who after marrying a Brahmin female convict lived in Andaman for 18 years (Rashida, 1998). However, with time owing to the peculiar isolated insular circumstances in which the convicts lived, the process of natural de-radicalisation ensued which aided in bringing forth the feeling of religious accommodation.

The colonialists in the Islands kept prisoners from different communities with each other so that they should not mix with their co-religionists and hatch conspiracies. As in mainland India, in Andaman too the British employed the divide-and-spy tactic to divide the communities and to create a loyal subservient class for themselves. The conditions under which the people lived were so artificial and much unlike those of ordinary communities that it was impossible to describe them on the usual lines (Imperial Gazetteer, 1994). This remark aims at the description of social state of convicts and the unofficial population in the regulated conditions of life imposed on them. The restrictions under which the free residents live have a distinct effect on the characters of those subjected to them from childhood to death. This effect became more and more apparent as generations after generation of convicts' descendents come under their pressure (Imperial Gazetteer, 1994).

In the colonial worldview India was a collection of the communities: self contained, inviolable groups and subgroups based on religion, profession and race (Risely, 1969). Caste and religion initially took a special importance to the penal society of Andaman for two primary reasons. First, the colony was founded in the wake of the Mutiny of 1857 which had the issues of religious sensibilities like greased cartridges. The colonialists therefore were particular about the social sensibilities of the prisoners and took care of not offending them. Secondly, given the British perception of the Indian society, it was inconceivable that a viable society of Indians could be constructed in the Islands without reference to caste and religion and application of segregation based on those criteria (Sen, 2000). While the British wanted to take all the social divisions into account in the construction of the penal society but they wanted to avoid the complexities of mainland. They reworked the social structure on the lines of administrative conveniences cutting the divisions down to the basic groups dictated by their comprehension of the Indian society. In fact, they recreated the workable social set up. As such religion became purely a personal affair in the Islands. Resultantly the ANI grew very rapidly into a very homogeneous society. However, there remained an unresolved contradiction between the vision of Andaman as a model colonial society and the view that the Islands were a dumping ground of the mainland refuse (Sen, 2000).

This workable set up with limited recourse to communal affiliations ultimately forged fundamentals of the Island's society.

Why and What For

From theorisation of diverse phenomena which Andaman and Nicobar Islands underwent since the penalisation days and forging of communal amity draws some possible answers. It is believed that the common and shared miseries are more unifying forces then the shared happiness and celebrations. The people of Andaman and Nicobar Islands have seen the dark days of penalisation under the British and even darker under the Japanese regime. Extreme conditions of terror, starvation and deprivation that prevailed diluted the barriers of religion. This had a solidifying effect on the fraternal bondage of the people of diverse ethnicities and religions. The people owing to their long distance from the mainland India have developed kind of emotional linkages which comes naturally to the people living in isolation from their native places. This process of integration of a variety of religious groups has produced a most interesting community of people with remarkable quickness of intellect and practical sense (Interview with RSS Ashish Mondal, 2015). The growth in immensity of solitude and separation has resulted in the formation socio-cultural economy with original bias towards newness. This has given rise to a great fusion phenomenon where almost everyone knows everyone.

The same geographical environment that people have to encounter has added to element of heterogeneous homogeneity. The natural calamities like cyclones and tsunamis which are a regular feature of the Islands' climatic calendar also aids in the consolidation of these fraternal bonds. In the disaster like situations the help from the mainland which often takes time to reach presses the people to reach for each other. Another strange but seemingly a valid point is the absence of strong regional political influence over the people. This may be due to the absence of provincial legislature and the regional political parties, though the parliamentary elections are fought enthusiastically. The fissiparous tendencies that regional power politics brings in its wake between the castes, religions, linguistic groups etc. are seemingly less crystallised in these Islands.

As in mainland India the evils of vote bank politics and tendencies of the religious groups to affiliate with one or the other political party is discernibly less concretised.

In spite of the composite culture that apparently harks on harmony there are certain silent undercurrents in the society depicting radicalising trends. It is being observed that due to unsolicited migrations much of which is illegal has placed more emphasis on overt religious markers. It is seemingly becoming more pronounced among the Muslim community begetting reactions from the sections of the Hindu community (Interview with RSS Ashish Mondal, 2015). As one communalism feeds on the other therefore hardening of stances have become more vehement. As far as the locals of both the communities are concerned they still nurture the values of tolerance and mutual accommodation. But increasing influx of outsiders primarily of religio-cultural backgrounds has subtly altered the harmonious communal equilibrium. The religion which used to be a personal affair is increasingly becoming a communal affair. Despite the dynamics of social change playing its role, the communal climate of ANI is far conducive to plural human growth in comparison to any other part of India.

Conclusion

In today's age of terror it is not unusual for a multi-religious and multi-ethnic society that Andaman is to feel vulnerable of social fragmentations. Of late, there are some discernible trends pointing towards the attempts at radicalisation of society. This holds a bit of truth in the wake of purported illegal influx of Bangladeshis and subtle efforts to alter the demographic profile of these Islands (Interview with IB official, 2015). Still, in Andaman and Nicobar Islands there seems the co-existence of old nativist ethno-communal traditions as well as the invented practices which are forged after migration to this place by the diverse people. The old traditions have made people wedded to their mainland roots and fostered the familial bondage among them. The invented ones whilst making people adaptable to the new homeland have encouraged and inculcated the *esprit de corps* in adjunct to communitarianism, rights and duties. The significant element that could be clearly demarcated is the fuzzy universalism of nationalism, sub-nationalism (Island nationalism), emoticons (emotional icons) and near preponderance of accommodative ideologies of Hinduism and Islam. So far the people have not allowed their religion to interfere in the secular communitarian life. The biggest gain that generates from studying such invented traditions is the understanding and interpretation of the people's past with the people's present, a transformation from penal society to a civil society. The evolution of peculiar communal traditions in a laboratory like atmosphere with historical and geographical interventions demonstrates how a secular state is achieved on plurality.

The Emerald Isles, as Andaman and Nicobar Islands are fondly called presents a place having markedly different inter-communal societal relations in relation to the mainland India. Separated by the 1200 kilometres of water body called the Bay of Bengal, these Islands present a picture perfect mini India albeit without associated disharmony. Over the years the insurmountable distance from the mainland India, close contact among themselves, compulsion of undergoing rigorous life, absence of religious diktats have forced the humans to defy the stigmas of caste, creed and provincialism and a unique society was in the offing (Roychowdhury, 2011). What is preached passionately in the mainland is practiced effortlessly here making the reading of Hindu-Muslim community an interesting research.

The society in the Andaman and Nicobar Islands has *prima facie* defied the cultural limitations. It overtly suggests that communication across traditions and cultures do not pose many problems when the meanings are general as well as universal. The pivotal component come across has been the innovation of emotionally and symbolically charged gestures of imperceptible universality (Eric, 1995). The rootlessness of a being which otherwise may undermine the conscious and belittle the morale, has played a constructive role here. The common background of the early settlers and their descendents and uniformity of future interests have united them as homogeneous group of people. The religion which supposedly has emerged as one of the greatest divisive forces of history has unwittingly played a stabilising role in the society which apparently is tremendously religious. The trends and relations may change sometime in future due to the forces of modernity and the present tradition of bonhomie and that of everyone knows everyone may no longer remain valid. Till the arrival of those times the rest of India may take a lesson or two from the Islanders.

NOTES

1. (The author in this very recent study explored the Hindu-Muslim relations in the medieval times particularly during the high time of Mughals and tried to show that there was great cross cultural interaction and admiration of each others' scholarship rather than much touted endemic conflicts).
2. (Interview with the RSS *vibhag pracharak* Ashish Mondal on 30 September, 2015. There was also an instance of a Government official named Majid in Andaman and Nicobar Islands who after independence was accused of trying to resettle 500 to 600 Muslims from East Bengal and therefore was suspected of trying to create an imbalance between Hindu and Muslim population and also of trying to ensure that Muslims became a majority. This instance is detailed in Iqbal N Singh, *op. cit.,* p. 282.
3. Interview with an Intelligence Bureau official on 25th September, 2015.)

REFERENCES

Brass, Paul R. (2003), *The Production of Hindu-Muslim Violence in Contemporary India*. Washington, University of Washington Press.

Chandramouli, C. (2013), *Census of India 2001, Primary Census Abstract, Total Population.Table 1-A Indian Series-1*, Office of the Registrar General and Census Commissioner, India, New Delhi.

Haughton to Home Department, 29 November, 1859, Government of India Home (Judicial), New Delhi, National Archives of India.

Hobsbawm, Eric (1995), "Introduction: Inventing Traditions", In Eric Hobsbawm and Terrence Ranger (ed.), *The Invention of Tradition.* Cambridge: Cambridge University Press.

Imperial Gazetteer of India Provincial Series, Andaman and Nicobar Islands (1994 Reprinted), New Delhi, Asian Educational Series.

Iqbal, Rashida *et. al*. (1998), *Who's Who*? Port Blair, Directorate of Education and Culture, Andaman and Nicobar Administration.

Khan, Iar Ali and S.N.H. Rizvi (2014). *The Locals of Port Blair: A Bio-Cultural Profile.* Delhi, B.R. Publishing Corporation.

Risely, H.H. (1969), *The People of India*, Delhi.

Roychowdhury, Rabin (2011), *The Untold Andaman and Nicobar Islands*. New Delhi, Manas Publications.

Sen, Satadru (2000), *Disciplining Punishment: Colonialism and Convict Society in Andaman Islands,* New Delhi, Oxford University Press.

Singh, N. Iqbal (1978), *The Andaman Story*. New Delhi, Vikas Publishing House.

Sinha, Surajit Chandra (1952), *Report on Survey of Further Possibilities of Resettlement: January-May 1952*. Resettlement of East Pakistan Refugees in Andaman Islands. Alipore, West Bengal Government Press.

Truschke, Audrey (2015), *Culture of Encounters: Sanskrit at the Mughal Court.* New York, Columbia University Press.

www.francoisgautier.com, *The Unknown Similarities between Hinduism and Islam.* Retrieved on 28.10.2015.

11

Growth of Muslim Society in Andaman and Nicobar Islands : A Historical Perspective

T. Prasad Rao

The release of data on Population by Religion Communities, 2011 in September 2015 brought about strange reactions from the different sections of Indian society, under mining the reasons, causes and rationalism in understanding the data. The fall in the Hindu Population by 0.7 percent to the total population and rise of the Muslim Population by 0.8 percent to the total population and register of growth rate of 16.8 percent among Hindus and 24.6 percent among Muslims. This is not the new trend, as growth of population is due to various social and economic factors rather than religion. International conference on Population and Development, Cairo in 1994 and Sachar Committee Report, 2005 viewed that any increase or decrease in population depends on various socio-economic indicators. Today we accept the idea that "Development as the best pill" to check population growth.

The above said determinant factors can be seen in operation, when we try to understand the growth of Muslim society in Andaman and Nicobar Islands.

The present settlement of Andaman and Nicobar Islands can be dated back to 1858, when it was brought under the colonial rule by establishing the Penal Settlement at Port Blair. This penal settlement was used for the deportation of political and criminal convicts for serving long term or life sentences, which was next to death sentence in British India Penal Code. Not only from the British India even convicts were deported from the Indian Native states on the payment basis to serve various punishments, imposed by the Native law courts up to 1938. In post-independence period, these islands were rehabilitated by East Pakistan refugees, settlers, contract labourers and other immigrants from time to time. So these islands had witnessed the implantation of the new social order different from the mainland India. The people of different regions, religions, languages, castes, nationalities and cultures moved on to these islands, leaving aside the cultural ethos of the mainland India and mixed among themselves without any distinctions of religion, caste, region, language, race and so on, to create a cosmopolitan society of its own.

Since the beginning of the settlement in Port Blair from 1858, Muslim community constituted an important component of immigrated population in Andaman and Nicobar Islands. The well known and influential members of Muslim community consisting of rulers, ministers, army generals, statesmen, *Zamindars, Ulema* and *Mulvis* from different parts of the Indian Sub-continent were deported to Andaman Penal Settlement as the Mutineers of 1857 rebellion, who were treated like common criminal convicts, later given due regard and looked upon with great respect by the local people. To name some, Fazlul Huq (*Maulavi* from Khairabad), Liaqat Ali (*Maulivi* from Allahabad), Syed Allauddin Hyderi (*Maulavi* of Hyderabad Deccan), Mir Jafar Ali Thaneswari and many more (Mujtaba and Mustaba, 2004). The Muslim society initiated by the learned and pious men from different parts of India, had an everlasting positive impact on these islands.

Deportation of Wahabi Rebels, who waged war against British Empire, under Ambala trial (1864), Patna trial (1865), Malda trial (1870) and Rajmal trial (1870) (Wababi Movement) to Andamans was another important event, which brought idea of *jihad* and radicalisation of Muslims in Andamans. Assassination of Viceroy Lord Mayo by Sher Ali in 1872 was viewed as an influence of Wahabi ideas.

Religion was never taken into consideration in the process of selection of convicts for transportation to Andaman Penal Settlement, the age below 45 years and good health, fit for labour were the conditions, certified by Surgeon at Alipore jail, before sailing to *Kalapani* from Calcutta (Home Department Proceeding, 1876). As elsewhere, in Port Blair, the great restore of those desiring to raise their social status is the adoption of Islam. As any 'self-supporter' can marry convict women from the female jail, with the permission of the settlement authorities had led to certain conversions to Islam, as Hindu would not be allowed to marry a Muhammadan women and vice versa.

Until 1881, under the pressure of the dominating conditions, the rule was merely Hindu to Hindu, Muhammadan to Muhammadan, Christian to Christian and so on. It is interesting to note that the caste or religion of the father was taken into consideration, ignoring that of mothers as a patriarchal practice (Imperial Gazetteer, 1908). Mr. Mustafa A.M, a senior citizen of Port Blair testify that his Grandfather *Pandit* Ayodiya Rai Sharma, S/o Pandit Jeevan Rai Sharma, R/o Kothar (Village), Shajahanpur (District) in Uttar Pradesh, who exiled to Andamans in 1871 for life, embraced Islam on his release as a "Free Convict" in 1891, subsequently known by name Nazir Mohammed, who left this mortal world on 23rd June 1923 (personal testimony of MA Mujtaba). The total convict population by 31st March 1892 was recorded as 11,356 at Port Blair Penal Settlement, of which Muhammadans numbered for 2,968 accounting for 26.14 percent (Report on The Administration, Port Blair for the year 1891-92).

Table 11.1: Growth of Muslim Population in Andaman and Nicobar Islands

Sl.No	Census Year	Total Population	Muslim Population	Percentage of Muslim Population	Growth Rate of Muslim Population
1	1901	24,649	4,207	17.07	---
2	1911	26,459	4,580	17.31	+0.24
3	1921	27,086	4,104	15.15	-2.16
4	1931	29,463	6,719	22.80	+7.65
5	1951	30,971	4,783	15.44	-7.36
6	1961	63,548	7,398	11.64	-3.80
7	1971	1,15,133	11,655	10.12	-1.52
8	1981	1,88,741	16,188	8.58	-1.54
9	1991	2,80,661	21,354	8.58	0
10	2001	3,56,152	29,265	8.22	-0.36
11	2011	3,79,944	32,371	8.52	+0.30

Source: Statistics out-line of Andaman and Nicobar Islands, Director of Statistics and Economics, Port Blair, Andaman and Nicobar Administration.

In the period of 1901 and 1911 the percentage of Muslim population was 17.07 percent and 17.31 percent to the total population of Andaman and Nicobar Islands respectively (Lowis, 1923).

The shift can be noticed from 1921, when the decision of abolition of Penal Settlement was taken by the British Government of India based on the Jails Committee report, 1920. Convicts were repatriated to main land jails and no longer were convicts received into Andamans, leading to fall in the population in general and Muslims in particular to 15.15 percent in 1921, (Lowis, 1923).

The decision to continue the Penal Settlement by Sir Alexander Muddiman, Home Member of the Government of India, transportation of Moplahs to Andamans (1923-26), more in the form of settlement and rehabilitation of these islands, rather than as a punishment led to rise in the percentage of Muslim population to 22.8 in Andaman and Nicobar Islands by 1931 (Lowis, 1911). Government started encouraging settlements in Andaman by giving grants of lands for 50 years to attract people from main land, sanction of agricultural tickets to 'Self-supporters' on large scale and self-supporters are encouraged to bring their families. The marginal rise of Muslim population by 2, 615 in number shows that, the growth is only due to coming of Malabar Moplah Muslims.

The evacuation of Andaman population on the eve of Japanese invasion in 1942 by British authorities and repatriation of people to mainland after independence in 1947 had led to fall in Muslim population to 4,783 in number, accounting for 15.44 percent of the total population by 1951 (Ghose, 1955). This indicates that Muslim population had taken great advantage of migrating to mainland India in the event of opportunity and crisis.

In the Post-Independent era, the need for building up population for the utilisation of the available land for agricultural purpose and for providing labour for the exploiting of the valuable forest, the displaced persons from East Pakistan were settled and the idea of colonisation of the islands was emerged. Between the period from

1949 to 1953, about 547 refugee families from East Pakistan were settled on the readily available, about 3000 acres of agricultural land, abandoned by the departing ex-convicts (Statistical Outline, Andaman and Nicobar Adminstration, 1962). The fall in the Muslim population to 11.64 percent and rise of Hindu population to 51.58 percent by 1961 (Sharma, 1964), clearly shows that immigrants are mostly Hindus.

With the intention of rehabilitate these islands in 1953, the Andaman and Nicobar Administration stated taking settlers into Andaman under Colonisation Scheme. Accordingly, agricultural families from different states were brought to these islands and allotted land for cultivation. Even under the Colonisation Scheme, the turnout of Muslim population into these islands was not significant, as the percentage of Muslim population was declined to 11.64 percent in 1961. About 3,281 families were settled under the Colonisation Schemes from East Bengal, Kerala, Madras, Mahe and Pondicherry, Burma evacuees and Chottanagpuri region during the First Five Years Plan (1951-56) and Second Five Years Plan (1956-61) (Statistical outline, 1961).

The Ministry of Rehabilitation, Government of India, had reintroduced the resettlement schemes in 1967 with a target to settle 10,000 families during fourth and fifth five year plans up to 1980. The entry of population in the form of settlers, contract labour, employees in various Government Departments, business and trade in post-independent era, had little impact on the growth of Muslim community in Andamans. The population of Muslims increased to 11, 655 in 1971 accounting to 10.12 percent of total Andaman and Nicobar Population, and in 1981 and 1991, the Muslim population had increased to 16,188 and 21,354 respectively, accounting for 8.58 percent in both the Census years.

The growth rate of Muslim population in Andaman and Nicobar Islands was recorded as zero during 1981-1991, it was-0.36 during 1991-2001 and a low growth rate of just 0.30 during 2001-2011, when compared to 32.9, 29.3 and 24.6 in the corresponding decadal years in India.

Table 11.2.: Decadal Growth Rate of Muslim Population in India and Andaman and Nicobar Islands During 1951-61 to 2001-2011.

Decadal years	1951-61	1961-71	1971-81	1981-91	1991-01	2001-11
India	24.43	31.2	30.8	32.9	29.3	24.6
Andaman and Nicobar Islands	-3.80	-1.52	-1.54	0	-0.36	0.30

The less growth rate of Muslim population in Andaman and Nicobar Islands can be attributed to their literacy level and economic wellbeing (Biswas, 2009). The literacy rate in these islands is one of the highest in India about 86.63 percent in total, 90.27 percent among the male and 82.43 percent among the female (Directorate of Economics and Statistics, 2014). The Gross enrolment ratio is 93.63 in 2011, which shows greater level of literary among the Muslims both in urban and rural areas in these islands. Along with the formal education the religious instructions are imparted by 22 *Madarasas* attached to the mosques mostly in South Andaman (Report on Performance and Functions of Waqf Board, 2015). Good literacy rate and education among the Muslims in these islands, led to better economic status with almost no Muslim family Below the Poverty Line (BPL), acts as the contraceptive to check the population growth rate in these island in general and Muslims in particular. The role of religion in growth of population can be ruled out by taking the reference of growth rate among the Muslims in Andaman and Nicobar Islands.

Islam among the Nicobaris, the native tribes of Nicobar Islands can be traced back to the Advent Minnicoyans in pre-British era and Muslim Gujarati merchants during British colonial period. Of late the number of Nicobari Muslims has increased in Car Nicobar and Nancowry Islands with the advent of R Akoojee Jadwet during the British period. At that time some Nicobari certainly showed interest in embracing Islam partly because they were eager to adopt outside cultural traits including food habits and partly because they were spiritually enlightened and had access to certain privileges. Later, they also encouraged others to become Muslims (Justine, 1992).

There is strong evidence that for a long time foreign nationals from Malaysia and Indonesia, who arrived on these tiny islands like Pilo-Milo, Kundul, Dering, Trinket in Nancowry group of Islands, were welcomed by local Nicobari families. Their frequent visits resulted in the establishment of intimate relations with local families as well as religious conversions (Biswas, 2015). Establishment of Malacca, Chuchukiya and Sawai Masjids in Nicobar Tehsil and Champion Masjid at Nancowry, Elahi and Pilpilow Masjids at Kamorta and Kapanga Masjid at Katchal in Nancowry Tehsil of Nicobar Islands, (Report on Performance and Function of Waqf Board, 2015) testify the propagation and practice of Islam in these remote islands which are not accessible to general non-tribal populations.

The Islamic community of Andaman and Nicobar islands give us completely a different and contrast image in comparison to mainland Indian scenario as projected in Sachar Committee report and Data on Population by Religion Communities, 2011. The study leads us to the following broad conclusion regarding the growth of Muslim community in these Bay Islands.

The Muslim population in pre-1920 era, mostly consisting of convicts and self-supporters accounted for more than 17 percent of the total population, above the National averages during the corresponding periods. Out word movement of Muslims from the islands had shown a up-ward trend, in the times of evacuation or repatriation in 1921, 1942 and 1947, leading to fall in the Muslim population in these islands.

Muslim inflow/immigration into these islands is limited, as a settlers or contract labourers in the post-independent era, through Colonisation Schemes, almost showing no impact on size and growth of Muslim population in these islands.

Like other parts of India, the conversion to Islam is very much limited among the tribals of Andaman and Nicobar Islands, except the some number in Nicobar Islands, under the influence of Muslim Gujarati traders in the region.

The better economic and educational status among the Muslims of Andaman and Nicobar Islands, had acted as a "Contraceptive pill" in checking the growth rate of Muslim population in Andaman and Nicobar Islands from 1970.

Andaman and Nicobar Islands present a unique model of communal harmony, with less importance to religious differences among its population. Inter-religious marriages are the common feature in these islands, with or without conversions, as the historical legacy of Penal Settlement. All religious festivals and ceremonies are celebrated by all the communities in harmony and communal differences are not known in these islands. Andaman and Nicobar islands are portrayed as a miniature of Indian sub-continent, without any communal aggressiveness and divisions. The Andaman and Nicobar Islands society can be adopted as a social model to promote communal harmony in Indian mainland.

REFERENCES

Basic Statistics of Andaman and Nicobar Islands-2013-14, *Director of Economic and Statistics, Andaman and Nicobar Administration*, , PDF format, Port Blair 2014.

Biswas, Swapan K. (2009), '*Colonisation and Rehabilitations in Andaman and Nicobar Islands*, New Delhi, Abhijeet Publications.

Biswas, Swapan K. (2015), 'Interreligious Marriage in Nicobar Islands Opportunities and Challenges', *Economic and Political Weekly,* Vol. L, No. 22, May 30, 2015.

Ghose, A.K., 'Census of India, 1951– the Andaman and Nicobar islands', Manager of Publication, Delhi, 1955.

Home Department Proceedings, September 1876, Port Blair – 'Selection of Convicts for Transportation to Andamans'.

Imperial Gazetter of India – Provincial Series of Andaman and Nicobar Islands, Calcutta, Superintendent of Government Printing, India, 1909.

Justine, Anstice, (1992), '*The Nicobarese'* (ed) K.S. Singh, Calcutta, Seagull Books, 1990.

Lowis, R.F. (1913), 'Census of India, 1911 – The Andaman and Nicobar islands', Calcutta, Superintendent Government Printing, India.

Lowis, R.F. (1923),'Census of India, 1921 – the Andaman and Nicobar islands', Calcutta, Superintendent Government Printing, India.

Mujtaba, M.A. and Mustafa, A.M., (2004), *'The Silent Past of Andamans: A Few Freedom Fighters of 1857'*, Port Blair, GCM Press.

Personal Testimony of Mr. Mustafa, A.M. (Retd.) Principal, Scholar and Senior Citizen of Port Blair.

Sharma S.K.(1964), 'Census of India, 1961 – Andaman and Nicobar Islands', Vol. XVII, Government Press.

Andaman and Nicobar Administration (1962), Statistical out-line of Andaman and Nicobar Islands Statistical Bureau, Port Blair, Government Press.

Andaman and Nicobar Administration, (1961), Statistical out-line of Andaman and Nicobar Islands, Statistical Bureau, Port Blair, Government Press.

The Report on the Administration of Port Blair for the year 1891-92, dated 9th November, 1892, Cellular Jail National Memorial Library, Port Blair.

Waqf, Board (2015), 'Report on Performance and Functions of Waqf Board (2009-2015)', Port Blair, Andaman and Nicobar Islands, Port Blair, Annexure-W.1.

Census of India, 1911-1913, 'The Andaman and Nicobar islands', Calcutta, Superintendent Government Printing India.

Waqf, Board (2015), 'Report on Performance and Functions of Waqf Board (2009-2015)', Port Blair, Andaman and Nicobar Islands, Annexure-V. 1-4.

Part-Four
Economy and Educational Perception in Islands Muslims

12

Socio-Economic Condition of Muslim Population in Andaman and Nicobar Islands : A Case Study of Immigrants from Bihar and West Bengal

Sushim Kumar Biswas

Introduction

Prior to 1788, the history of Andaman and Nicobar Islands was centred on the aboriginals only and the literature survey reveals that there was no concrete, robust and chronological record available. The substantiated facts of Andaman Islands began to come to notice only after the arrival of Lieutenant Archibald Blair in 1789 with the objective of hydrographic survey of these Islands in compliance of the instructions of the Governor General of India, Lord Cornwallis. On the basis of his report, a settlement comprising about 200 mechanics, craftsmen, Sepoys, and labourers, was born in September 1789. By 1791, the settlers started bringing their families from mainland. However, the settlement was abandoned in May 1796 because of adverse circumstances being faced by them. The 270 convicts and 550 free men, women and children were shifted back. The religion-wise number of population was not indicated there. The first phase of history of these Islands came to an end here.

The second phase of history was started on 22nd January, 1858, when Captain Man raised the Union Jack at Port Blair for the second time with the objective of Penal Settlement. The concept of Penal Settlement was conceived of by the British authority due to many reasons. The most important reason was that there was lack of jail accommodation in mainland of India as the number of convicts was on the increasing trend at that time because of mutiny against British administration in India. Thereafter, the Penal Settlement remained unabated along with a series of events over time and was ultimately abolished in 1945 during Japanese occupation. The religion-wise number of population was also not indicated in the second phase of the history of Penal Settlement. However, it is worthwhile to mention the name of a Pathan convict, Sher Ali, who had assassinated the then Viceroy and Governor-General of India, Lord Mayo, who came to these Islands to take stock of Penal Settlement. The author of Pen Pictures of the Andaman and Nicobar Islands, S. Y. Yusuf Hussain, vividly explained the character of Sher Ali. In an autobiography in Urdu written by Maulana Mohammad Jafar Thanesvri, who was also in the Andamans at that time as one of the transportees, the incident of assassination by Sher Ali and his attitude towards this act was captured in a fantastic way. Therefore, it may be presumed that there was no doubt about the existence of Muslim population in the Penal Settlement of second phase. However, the exact number of Muslim population is available only from the Census of India beginning from 1901.

So far as this study is concerned with the socio-economic condition of Muslim population, it becomes imperative to mention the rebellion of Moplahs and their arrival in Andamans. Since ancient times, Malabar was known as the traditional centre for trade in pepper. Sometime in ninth century, a number of Arab Muslims came and actually settled in Malabar. They got married to local Dravidian women, which gave birth to a new community to be known as Moplah. They were involved with Khilafat movement and they believed that the British were against Islam and Hindus were infidels (kaffirs). Ultimately, the movement turned primarily anti-Hindu. On 25th July, 1921, a clash with the police in which

5000 Moplahs were involved, took place tremendously. But once again the British won the battle and the Moplahs were, after trial, sentenced to transportation. Thus, the Moplah community formed in these Islands. It was predicted that a group of 1400 in number were sent to the Andamans as prisoners and they were allowed to live with their families and a new experiment, of allowing them to live in separate villages, was tried. Their acculturation and adaptation with this environment took place quickly because of its similarity to that of their original home in the Malabar. They were able to achieve economic independence quickly because of their industrious nature and skill in crafts. Needless to say that presently this community plays an important role in the economic development of these Islands. In spite of being a minority community, their contribution to GSDP is, no doubt, too high in comparison to other communities of these Islands. But, no attempt has been undertaken to substantiate this fact in this study.

A remarkable ethnicity and cultural diversity among the population of Andaman and Nicobar Islands is discernible. The entire population can be divided into three categories – tribal population, descendants of criminals under sentence of transportation for life from India and Burma, and settlers under Rehabilitation Scheme. Apart from these, there is one more category that can be termed as recent immigrants from different states of India. Since the demand for labour is more than its existing supply in these Islands, the arrival of people from various parts of India remained unabated to find job in organised as well as in unorganised sector. The contribution of these people constitutes an important factor towards the development of these Islands. The most recent immigration of Muslim population in these Islands from the District of North 24 Parganas in West Bengal and Bihar has been the subject matter of this study. Till now, no study has been undertaken to study the socio-economic condition of these people in these Islands. There is no doubt that an improved mode of socio-economic condition is positively correlated with the productivity of workers. Since their participation in economically gainful activities of these Islands has become so significant, it becomes imperative to pay attention towards the study of the socio-economic condition of these people and accordingly, an attempt has been made in this paper.

Materials and Methods

A detail observation on the socio-economic condition of the immigrants of Muslim population has been carried out in two locations, viz. Dairy Farm and Mohanpura, where they live in clustered form. Most of the Bengali Muslim families who came from the District of North 24 Parganas of West Bengal adjacent to Bangladesh border use to live in two pockets of Port Blair Municipal area in clustered form – Dairy Farm and Junglighat. However, those Muslim people who have come alone leaving their families in the hometown are found sporadically everywhere from the extreme south to the extreme north of these Islands, but mostly confined in South Andaman District. Apart from it, a group of Muslim people who came from Medinipur District of West Bengal is engaged with the activity of plumbing, but their nature and characteristics are different from the above group. On the other hand, a large number of Muslim people who came from Bihar are mainly engaged with the retail selling of fruits and they use to live in and around market area in clustered form. In addition, some people of Sivan District of Bihar are engaged in hair dressing business and like to stay in the heart of the town. Data for the present study had been collected on complete enumeration from the study area. A set of questionnaire were interviewed with almost all the people of Dairy Farm and all the fruit sellers to assess their various socio-economic parameter like health, income level, indebtedness, family size and literacy level, etc. Data collected on different aspects of socio-economic status of these people in study area has been analysed by different statistical tests like average and correlation coefficient. The outcome of these tests could be utilised for formulating policies of this weaker section of the community and will cater as backup for identification of target people for implementing different Government programmes.

Results

Reasons for Immigration

The reasons for immigration of Muslim population from the District of North 24 Parganas are abject poverty, indebtedness, lack of social security, low level of social status, lack of employment opportunities, political turbulence, lack of credit facilities, exploitation by muscle power, etc. On the other hand, the reason for immigration of Muslim population from Bihar is mainly due to lack of regular employment opportunities and severe competition in business and other allied activities.

Economic Activities and Income

The activities performed by the immigrant Muslim people from West Bengal can be divided into three categories – (i) construction workers, (ii) maid-servants, and (iii) sellers of *golgappa* (*pani puri*) and rice flakes. Most of the people are working as labourers in construction sector and presently they are paid at the rate of Rs. 400-Rs. 500 per day which is much higher than the minimum wage rate. The inflow of these people in Andaman has increased rapidly only after the devastating Tsunami which struck on 26th December, 2004. In order to regain the infrastructural development, the money supply has increased in huge amount in these Islands. But the shortfall of workers has induced the contractors to bring man power from mainland. As the cost of living is too high here, the female members have been working as maid servants to supplement the family's income. Thus, a separate sector of economic activity has developed and prior to their arrival, this sector was least important. The income of maid servants varies from person to person depending upon their efficiency and availability of work at suitable place. It is observed that their monthly income ranges from Rs. 3000 to Rs. 5000. A few of these people is engaged with the activity of making *golgappa* (*pani puri*) and selling it at roadside. The earning of these people is above Rs. 10,000 per month. Besides this, a few people mostly below 14 years is engaged with the activity of selling spicy rice flakes at various places including park, places adjacent to school and college, etc. It is observed from an oral interview that a group comprising more than 200 people who came from Egra of Medinipur District of West Bengal is working as plumbers and their monthly income is nearly Rs. 15,000 and they use to remit approximately Rs. 10,000 per month to their family members in mainland.

On the other hand, the main activity of Muslim immigrants who came from Bihar in the 80s and 90s mostly belonging to Patna District is retail business of fruits selling and their minimum earning on an average is Rs. 15,000 per month. This is worth noting that the immigrant Muslim women of West Bengal are working as maid servants, whereas it is not found at all in the immigrant Muslim women of Bihar. Besides this, a few people from Sivan District is running men's parlour (hair-dressing) in and around the Port Blair town and they earn more than Rs. 15, 000 per month.

From the present observation, an attempt has been made to show that income of a family is the most important index for getting an idea about the socio-economic condition of this community. Here their income depends on various parameters such as adaptation, efficiency, communication skill, honesty, weather, employment at suitable place, attitude of the employer, frequency of visiting home town, etc. However, an equitable distribution of income is observed among those who are engaged in construction sector. But, income distribution shows significant inequality among the maid servants, fruit sellers and those who are engaged in allied activities.

Literacy Level

Education becomes imperative to human life. Education is an instrument of social change and transformation. It transforms the human resource into human capital, which in turn, enhances the productivity. It helps women to overcome the social, cultural and psychological barriers and enables them to participate as equal partners in development. The rate of literacy has been observed to be very frustrating. Among the literates, the maximum number has hardly completed primary level education while the rest dropout before completing primary education. It is observed that the literacy rate of women is almost negligible because most of this community has a positive attitude about education of their male children but female education beyond. It is largely due to rampant poverty, ignorance, superstition, lack of awareness, early marriage and lack of social security for female children.

It is observed from the study that most of this community wants their children to receive education so that they can have a better job and thus improve their social and economic status. But often they cannot help but pull their children out from the school and engage them in some economic activity to supplement their family income. However, as they are influenced by the prevailing environment and demonstration effect, they have changed their mentality a full circle and consequently they also use to send their children to Government School where free education along with free mid-day meal is provided. Some of them are also studying in local colleges and a few is so meritorious that they have got the opportunity of studying technical and non-technical courses in premier institutes like NIIT in mainland. Since there are immense opportunities of getting education free of cost along with various incentives, the children of this community are attracted towards availing this facility in these Islands.

Housing Condition and Family Size

Living standard of this community is not as good as the cost of living is too high in these Islands. Almost all the people live in rental houses which are closely constructed. These houses are not so spacious and in most of the cases having no drainage facilities. So far as the Bihari Muslims are concerned, the monthly rent paid by them varies from Rs. 2500 to Rs. 5000 depending upon the earning of the family. The average family size of the study area is found to consist of eight members. The per-head availability of space is much smaller than requirement. Most of the households are nuclear type, but they are having joint family system in mainland. Women and children also help them in business in the domestic front and women are basically engaged in the maintenance of house. The authority of women in households, their freedom of movement, their economic, educational and other opportunities are not at all satisfactory and they have a much lower status than that of the men in the social hierarchy. However, it needs to be mentioned that their standard of living here is much better than that of mainland. A gradual social transformation in all respects is taking place and psychological barrier is removing over time.

On the other hand, the rent paid by the Bengali Muslims ranges between Rs. 2000 to Rs. 3500 depending upon the earning as well as family size. The average family size of the study area is found to consist of five members, which is much lower than the Bihari family. The authority of women is similar to that of Bihari Muslims.

Indebtedness

Indebtedness is considered one of the indicators of poverty meant for the poor people, which in turn become the vicious circle for them. It is observed from the study area that so far as the Bengali Muslim is concerned, the most important reason of their immigration being the abject poverty and indebtedness. Almost all of them have taken loan from the moneylenders at exorbitant rate of interest by mortgaging their property for the purpose of construction of house, daughter's marriage, small business, farming, etc. Later they become unable to repay the loan because of non-availability of job opportunities and huge loss in small business, rather they are forced to take loan again and ultimately they become bankrupted gradually. As the demand for labour as well as the wage rate is too high in these Islands, the amount of earning here makes them able to repay loan in mainland and get back their property. Not only that, there are some people who have been able to purchase landed property and construct residential house in their native place.

On the other hand, the economic condition of Bihari Muslims is better than that of Bengali Muslims. Almost all the Bihari Muslims have their landed property and houses in mainland. The main reason for their immigration is to engage them in regular income earning activity so that they can send money to their family members to maintain and expand property.

Health Hazards

The study reveals that they have been facing health and hygienic problem also. As most of the Bengali Muslims are engaged in construction sector, their working environment is not so good. Very often they suffer from diarrhea, gastro-intestinal disorders, malaria, typhoid, scabies, and particularly infectious and skin diseases. The main reasons are unhealthy feeding habit and habitation and un-hygienic condition. Most of the people are ignorant of the quality and quantity of the food to be taken at different times in a day. Mostly they cook once in a day and consume it all along the day and that too does not conform to the balanced diet. They live in small low-cost houses having no drainage facilities and no approach road except narrow footpath. Some of them who are living in *kutcha* and semi-*pucca* houses are not having bathroom and latrine facilities.

Acculturation

The base word of acculturation is 'culture'. Culture means a way of living and a way of life, which include learning a new language, immersion, assimilation and integration. Language and immersion are the most important parts of the acculturation process. In order to adapt a new culture, one needs to learn a new language. One of the most effective ways to learn a new language is through immersion, or surrounding yourself entirely in a new culture. Assimilation involves the accumulation of information about a new culture and resulting adaptations to match the new culture. Integration means participation in societal events by the immigrants in order to emulate themselves in the society. All the immigrants from West Bengal and Bihar, are already acquainted with the colloquial language of these Islands. As a result, they are able to understand the customs, traditions, acceptable behaviours and so on. As there is co-existence of people from all states of Indian Union irrespective of caste, creed and religion, the processes of assimilation and integration do not take much time for them to experience the entire acculturation process.

Social Status

The social status which they are enjoying here is presumed to be at par with the people of these Islands. The Andaman and Nicobar Islands is a miniature form of India and the peaceful co-existence of people from all provinces irrespective of caste, creed, and race is an exemplary. Freedom of participation of people from all communities in social, religious and cultural events is discernible. When a person is given due status, dignity and importance, he becomes a responsible contributor towards the society where he lives. That is why the poor and neglected immigrants minorities from mainland like to settle in these Islands.

Discussion

The results of the correlation analysis clearly reveal that income and family size is positively correlated to each other and also shows positive correlation on the Income and Investment. The positive correlation clearly envisages that the more the family size, the more will be the family income. Though, the family size and monthly income varies among the Bengali and Bihari Muslims. Because of the situation, the number of immigrants is increasing high day by day. Therefore, family size is an important factor in this study and maximum income means more strength of the household. Income is also interrelated with several other parameters like the consumption pattern, educational level, house type, occupational status and the general living conditions. So, income of a family is the most important index for getting an idea about the socio-economic condition of the people.

The report of the High-Level Committee under the chairmanship of Justice Rajindar Sachar to study the 'Social, Economic and Educational Status' of the Muslim Community of India is supposed to be a deviation with reference to that of the Muslim Community of Andaman and Nicobar Islands. The social, economic and educational status of Muslim Community of these Islands is considered at par with the people of other community. It is presumed that no separate mechanisms are required to ensure equity and equality of opportunity of this community. The contribution being made by them in all respects is an exemplary to those of their counterpart in mainland. However, the subject matter of present study is concerned with somewhat a different disadvantageous group of people of this community, who are the recent immigrants from mainland. As a result, their socio-economic condition is not at all comparable with that of permanent inhabitants of Muslim community of these Islands. But the existing mechanisms to ensure equity and equality of opportunity are also applicable for them. Needless to say that this group requires special attention and the recommendations made by the High-Level Committee will be beneficial for their upliftment.

REFERENCES

Das, S. T. (1982), *The Indian Islands* (*A Study of Habitat, Economy and Society*), New Delhi, Cosmo Publications.

Dhingra, K. (2005), *The Andaman and Nicobar Islands in the 20th Century – A Gazetteer*. New Delhi, Oxford University Press.

GOI, (2006), "Social, Economic and Educational Status of the Muslim Community of India – A Report", Prime Minister's High Level Committee, Cabinet Secretariat, Government of India (Chairperson-Justice Rajinder Sacher), New Delhi.

Khan, A. (2011), "Socio-economic Status of Muslims in Western U.P.", *The Indian Economic Review*, Vol. VIII (2), August.

Mondal, S.R. (2006), "Muslim Society and Culture in Bengal: Tradition and Change" in *Islam Muslim Communities in South Asia*, ed. N. Hasnain, New Delhi, Serials Publications.

Mondal, S.R. (1997), *Educational Status of Muslims: Problems, Prospects and Priorities*, New Delhi, Inter-India Publications.

Pandey, G.S. (1996), *Ross Island – The Headquarters of Indian Penal Settlement*. Port Blair, Sangeeta Publishing House.

Rahaman, M.T. and Bhuimali, A. (2011), *Indian Muslims and their Economy*. Delhi, Abhijit Publications.

Singh, N. Iqubal (1978), *The Andaman Story*. New Delhi, Vikas Publishing House.

Talib, P. (2012), "Educational Initiatives to Transform Muslim Community", in *Empowerment of Indian Muslims: Perspectives, Planning and Road Ahead*, eds. M.A. Beg and A.R. Kidwai, New Delhi, Concept Publishing Company.

Mathur, L. P. (1969), *History of Andaman and Nicobar Islands* (1756-1966). Delhi, Sterling Publishers.

Index

F

G

J

K